Individual Testimonials

The only thing that will change you from where you are today to where you will be five years from now are the people you meet, the dreams you dream, and the books you read. Read and study Bill Bartmann's book, *Billionaire Secrets To Success,* and you will change dramatically for the better.

Lou Holtz
Coach

Your story interested me to such an extent that I have taken the liberty to note your path to success in several speeches I have made since becoming Drake's president.

Robert D. Ray
President of Drake University—Former Governor of Iowa

Bill Bartmann has experienced more success and failure as an entrepreneur than anyone I know. He has the spirit of a champion and the heart of a teacher. Learn from his experience.

Jim Stovall
Emmy Award Winner,
President of Narrative Television Network and
Author of *The Ultimate Gift*

The mission Bill is living, born out of great personal pain to a man uniquely qualified to handle the difficult challenges, is destined to touch the lives of tens of millions of people who need the guidance of a skilled servant leader such as Bill.

Alexander J. Berardi
Author of *Never Offer Your Comb To A Bald Man*

I've never known anyone who could inspire and motivate people like Bill Bartmann. The man has an uncanny knack of making you believe you can do the impossible. It is not so much that you believe in him, you believe in his belief in you. He has an absolute conviction that people can be what they want to be and instills that confidence in others around him. It's a God given talent that is rarely seen in someone who truly cares about his fellow man.

Carol McCloud
Author of *Climbing Out*

People who try things in life often fail, and the ones I admire are the ones who fail and get back on the horse.

Cal Hobson
Senate Pro Tem

Bill Bartmann has a genuine enthusiasm that is contagious and inspiring. It is further enhanced by a deeply rooted desire to make a profoundly positive impact in the lives of individuals and organizations. He was able to motivate an army of people to exceed the expectations of themselves.

Dave Jewitt
President, Your One Degree

Bill is a real leader who has a knack to help people find their way through challenges. He works on ideas that fuel growth in the future, not today . . . then makes it happen by communicating and motivating.

Christine Cranke
Director of Operations, West Teleservices, Inc.

Over the years, in the UK and the USA, I have consulted with many companies in many industries. I have never seen anyone polarize, motivate, and lead with one-tenth the dedication and skill that Bill lavished on our 4,000 employees. Bill "tuned" our people to be a responsive team—the most successful our industry has ever seen.

Chris Horrocks
Chairman
Strategic Advanced Management Systems, Inc.
Barrington, IL

One of the problems with having been associated with Bill Bartmann is not only do you end up thinking you can fly off cliffs, you end up looking for cliffs to jump off just to prove you can fly. Guess what . . . you can!

Stephen R. Money JD
Chairman of the Board
AllCare Health Systems, Inc.
El Paso, TX

It's a unique human being who can build a business from nothing. Most of us are just waiting for that one great idea, and Bill's doing it time and time again.

Mickey Thompson
Chamber of Commerce

Bill is a true example of the survival of the human spirit! Bill has found another way to share his inspirational experiences. He exemplifies the entrepreneurial spirit, a rare gift in his magnitude.

Gabriele Blankenship
ADVO Inc.

Bill has reached revolutionary milestones in his many endeavors in life—both professionally and personally. Simply put, Bill Bartmann is a remarkable individual who has the gift of inspiring and motivating others with his wisdom.

Diana Hernandez
Training Development Specialist

Unlike most "experts," Bill has been there—and more than once! His teachings and ideas have helped me in my own career—to take chances, to rise above setbacks, and to set and reach goals. To me, Bill Bartmann is a teacher, a role-model, and, most importantly, an inspiration.

Betsy Hesselrode
JD Jackson, TN

As a professional in the financial industry, I look at Bill as an inspiration. I am using his management techniques every day to motivate my people. His passion for life and success has inspired me to be a leader in my company. A true pioneer, Bill has inspired thousands of people to succeed.

Jason Barry
Phoenix, AZ

Media Testimonials

Patron Saint of the Second Chance. A second chance. Who better to offer it than Bill Bartmann.

The Wall Street Journal

Bill Bartmann has built a big business of bad debt. He also may have made bill collectors kinder and gentler. And on the way, he became one of the USA's richest men. None of it would have happened if he hadn't gone broke.

USA Today

Bill Bartmann survived failure, remade one of the country's ugliest industries, and became a billionaire.

Inc. **Magazine**

Although Bartmann lost his company, he managed to turn his loss into an opportunity that made him a billionaire and changed an entire industry.

National Public Radio—Chris Arnold

Bartmann has leaped onto the Forbes 400 list, landed on the cover of *Inc.* magazine, and was among *BUSINESSWEEK's* Entrepreneurs of the Year.

BusinessWeek **Magazine**

Bartmann is a quintessentially American figure. Perhaps that is because he is fundamentally a pioneer and a frontiersman, a relentless optimist with unbounded self confidence. When he's down, he bounces back with a vengeance.

New Yorker **Magazine**

Bartmann's success is the stuff of the American Dream.

Barron's

Bill Bartmann is a populist capitalist. Bill Bartmann . . . put a seedy and inefficient industry on the road to respectability.

Fortune **Magazine**

Bartmann comes to success after experiencing his own hard times. In 1986, he was not only broke but $1 million in debt as a result of the bankruptcy of his oil business.

Entrepreneur Of the Year **Magazine**

Losing your shirt in the oil business isn't everyone's idea of an education. But for Bill Bartmann, the experience packed about a dissertation's worth of knowledge.

Asset Backed Securities Week

Bartmann's espousal of "humanitarian capitalism" grows out of the experiences of his youth.

Tulsa People **Magazine**

A bold and innovative example of doing not just what makes good business sense but also doing what is socially and morally right for a community, proving that the concepts are not mutually exclusive.

Urban Tulsa

One of the Phoenix 50 Entrepreneurs who crashed and burned—and bounced back stronger than ever.

Success **Magazine**

Bill is a very highly motivated entrepreneur attracted to the "mission impossible" scenario.

Tulsa Business Journal

Bill Bartmann is truly a man of vision. His vision is to create an economically successful enterprise by fighting for his customers and putting their true interest first. He believes that the best path to success is through improving the lives of others.

The Oklahoma Eagle

For some, real life can be more fascinating than fiction. Bill Bartmann is an engaging guest with an amazing life story.

Debra Woodall
Managing Editor, KRMG News
Tulsa, Oklahoma

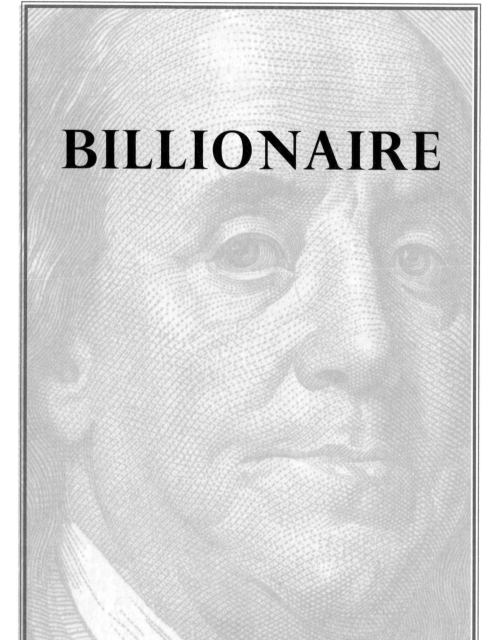

BILLIONAIRE

BILLIONAIRE

Secrets to Success

BY BILL BARTMANN

BILLIONAIRE
SECRETS TO SUCCESS

© 2005 Bill Bartmann

Written by Bill Bartmann.

Manufactured in the United States.

For information, please contact:
Brown Books Publishing Group
16200 North Dallas Parkway, Suite 170
Dallas, Texas 75248
www.brownbooks.com
972-381-0009
A New Era in Publishing™

Hardbound ISBN: 1-933285-31-1
LCCN 2005908462
2 3 4 5 6 7 8 9 10
Second Printing 2006

www.billbartmann.com

Dedication

This book is dedicated to my wife Kathy.

For the ten years we dated and the thirty-two we have been married, she has been my inspiration and my motivation. She has not only been the wind beneath my wings, she has been the hand gently placed upon my back. And when I get a little too full of myself, she is the swift kick in the pants I feel from time to time.

Her love, her guidance, and her support have always remained constant—in the best of times and, more importantly, in the worst of times.

Kathy and I met when I was fourteen and she was eleven. When she met me, I was a homeless high school dropout with plenty of bad habits and a very bad attitude. Somehow she saw more value and promise in me than I had ever seen. She has managed to transfer that high school dropout into whatever it is that I have become. All of my accomplishments—every one of them—are not mine at all, but rather, they are hers.

In addition to working her magic on me, she has done the same for our two wonderful daughters, Jessica and Meghan. She has raised, nurtured, and educated them—much of it, I am embarrassed to say, without my help or involvement. Both of our daughters have their mother's beauty, brains, and sense of who they are. At the end of my life, when I look back at the things of which I am the most proud, it won't be the awards, the accolades, or the money—it will be these three women: Kathy, Jessica, and Meghan.

Ladies, knowing you has made me the luckiest man on the face of the planet Earth.

Table of Contents

Preface

I may not know what the future holds—but I know who holds the future.

—Lou Holtz

Destiny is not a matter of chance; it is a matter of choice. It is not a thing to be waited for; it is a thing to be achieved.

—William Jennings Bryan

It is never too late to be what you might have been.

—George Elliott

*You have brains in your head.
You have feet in your shoes.
You can steer yourself any direction you choose.
You are on your own. And you know what you know.
And YOU are the guy who'll decide where to go.*

*—Dr. Seuss
Oh, the Places You'll Go!*

For I know the plans I have for you, declares the Lord. Plans to prosper you and not harm you, plans to give you hope and a future.

—Jeremiah 29:11

This book is dedicated solely to the task of explaining and teaching each person who reads it how to take control of his or her life and successfully accomplish any goal. This is a big promise. But it is also a promise that I guarantee will be delivered to each person who reads and follows the steps set forth in this book.

There have been hundreds of self-help books written in the past, and each of them has made some type of similar promise. These books generally fall into one of the following four categories:

1. **Academic Gymnastics:** Typically, these are the books written by psychologists, psychiatrists, or other academic professionals. While some of these may contain beneficial suggestions and ideas, they are so crammed with medical and psychological terminology that the average person gets lost trying to plow through it. These books may be great sources of information, but if the reader can't comprehend what the author is trying to communicate, all that wonderful research is wasted.

2. **Instant Experts:** Usually, these books are the type you see advertised on late-night television by someone who hasn't really succeeded at anything other than in his ability to sell the book he hopes will finally make him a success. These books are suspect. If the method works so well, why didn't the author succeed at something other than his own book sales? Maybe if these books just focused on how to write a book and sell it on late-night television, I would find them a little more credible.

3. **They Did It So You Can Too:** These books typically provide all sorts of emotional stories of great accomplishments performed by other people. While these stories can be inspirational (and inspiration is certainly

an important factor), without providing the proper guidance for you to be able to perform one of these wonderful accomplishments, this inspiration fades quickly.

Seven different authors have used stories about me in their books on success. While I am flattered to be so included, it doesn't necessarily establish the author as an authority on success, just because he or she can write about someone else's accomplishments.

4. **Trust Me—It Works:** These books generally tell you to engage in "positive thinking," develop a "positive mental attitude," or to "believe in yourself." Again, these are wonderful and important concepts, but these books fail to explain how and why the process works. The grand majority of people need to understand and feel comfortable with how something works before they will commit a strong belief in it. These books fail to explain how and why it works. Instead, they rely on the reader's accepting these concepts at face value. It is extremely difficult to have faith and bet your future on something you don't fully understand.

I am convinced that we can control our future. Although we can't always control the things that happen to us, we can control how we react and respond to the things that happen to us. By choosing how to react and respond to the things that happen to us, we do take control over our future.

This belief comes from the adoption of various principles I have found scattered throughout books like these. I have applied these principles to my own life as well as to those around me. As I tried to teach other people how to master this control, I became increasingly frustrated with the books that were available. None of them really explained the process or how to apply it to my own life. It was this frustration that caused me to write this book.

This book is different from the four types previously listed, in the following ways:

1. It is written in easy-to-understand language. It is written for the general public, not as a scientific-medical dissertation.

2. The principles of this book have been tested and have proven to work in my life as well as in others'. These nine principles are not the product of some academic conclusion. I have tested these nine principles, not once, not twice, not three times, but four times over the past twenty-five years, and they have worked every time.

3. This book does not require blind faith in anything. It will clearly and carefully explain how the human mind works and how we can use it to help us accomplish our goals.

4. In five easy-to-read chapters, this book will give you step-by-step guidelines to help you accomplish your goals by showing you how to improve your self-esteem, a crucial element in the process of achieving any goal.

Chapter One: Understanding the Process

This chapter explains how the human brain receives and processes information. Unless a person understands how and why this process works, he or she cannot maximize peak utilization from our most important personal resource: the mind itself. Ignorance of this process requires one to rely on vague concepts such as "faith" or "power of positive thinking."

While these are wonderfully productive tools for those who can accept them without understanding how they work, most people possess a deep inner need to understand something before they can accept it and believe in it. It is this oversight by authors of self-help books—explaining how the process actually works—that has caused so many people who have read their books to claim they don't work. The concepts do work but only if you accept and believe them. These authors have failed to recognize that we live in an era of unprecedented scientific and technological breakthroughs. These dramatic changes have caused society to become much more cause and effect oriented. We have come to understand that things do not just happen by themselves. We no longer believe that volcanoes erupt because the Gods are angry; we understand they are caused by the intense energy created by the shifting of tectonic plates.

Likewise, no one believes we put a man on the moon simply because we wished it. Instead, people know and understand that it took countless numbers of interdependent steps all working in a logical unison to make space flight a reality.

Although we may not have the same degree of knowledge of plate tectonics as a geophysicist, or the same degree of knowledge of space flight as an aeronautical engineer, we at least understand the concept and recognize that these things happen because of specific reasons. We also understand that if these same steps are repeated, the same result will follow. So it is with achieving success—if you follow the steps, the desired result will follow.

Accepting the power of positive thinking is no different. If we are to believe that it can work, we must first understand how it works. That doesn't mean we have to have the same degree of knowledge of the brain that a neurosurgeon has. It does mean, however, that we have to understand, at least in general terms, how this phenomenon is produced.

Chapter Two: Controlling the Process

Once we understand how the brain receives and processes the information that ultimately determines our success or failure, we can then ensure that it receives and processes only information that facilitates our goals and makes their accomplishment a virtual certainty. Chapter two also explains how we can control (and even manufacture) the information sent to our brain.

Chapter Three: Implementing the Process

Here you'll learn the specific steps necessary for consistent goal attainment. Once we understand how the brain works and then how to effectively control the information it will process, it is only a matter of applying these principles to achieve any goal we establish.

Chapter Four: Rigors of Exercise

The element most books on this topic tend to ignore is that achieving success requires effort! There is no secret potion nor is there a mystical incantation or a genie from a magic lamp that will provide success just because we wish it to be so. Although achieving success does require effort, it actually requires much less effort than most people use . . . to remain unsuccessful! This chapter explains how to focus your efforts toward your goal so that none of your energies are wasted. Effort without knowledge of how something works and/or a concrete plan to accomplish it is a waste of energy. Once you understand the process, all your effort can be focused on the specific target you have chosen.

Chapter Five: Change the Way You View Yourself

Chapter five explains how we can take the information learned in the first four chapters of this book and improve our self-esteem by changing the view our subconscious mind has of us. The easy-to-use worksheets help you identify and reinforce the positive experiences that have occurred in your life.

Once a person understands these principles and applies them to his or her daily life, an amazing transformation begins to occur.

To illustrate my point, let me describe someone I know.

He was born in the "flats" (a poor neighborhood near the meatpacking plant, junk yards, and railroad tracks).

He was one of eight children born to a janitor who never earned more than $6,000 a year. His mother cleaned other people's houses to help provide money for necessities.

He grew up eating food supplied by the government through the "Foodstuffs Commodity Program" (the forerunner of the food stamp program). Once a month, he would go with his father to the distribution center and stand in line to wait for the family's allotment of dried beans, canned meat, powdered milk, and processed cheese.

His family moved into eight different rent houses during the first fourteen years of his life. Some of these houses did not have indoor plumbing. Several of these moves were required because the city had condemned their former residence as unfit for human habitation.

He started smoking at age twelve, by stealing his father's cigarettes.

He was born with a hearing defect that went undiagnosed for the first seventeen years of his life. As a result, he could not and did not understand or follow directions or instructions in school. He quickly became labeled a problem student and a disciplinary problem.

As a grade school student, he was such a problem both in school and at home that his parents said they wished he were dead.

He weighed ninety-three pounds when he was in high school.

While in high school, he was such a disciplinary problem that he was expelled from two different schools. As a result of his perpetual suspensions and expulsions, he spent five and a half years in high school, yet never graduated. He didn't consider this such a big deal—no male member of his entire family tree had ever graduated from high school!

At age fourteen, he left home and said, "No one even noticed."

He joined a traveling carnival.

Later, he joined a street gang known as the "Manor Boys." A number of the members of this gang ended up using drugs, doing time in prison, or committing suicide.

He hid his insecurity by becoming a "tough guy"; he established his toughness by getting into fights as often as he could. Since he was the smallest member of his gang, he would go in first and start a fight by slugging the biggest guy in the rival group, causing them to chase him outside where the rest of his gang would be waiting.

At age seventeen, he tried to enlist in the Marine Corps and was rejected because of a hearing problem.

As a high school dropout, he went through a string of lousy jobs, including logging, laying sod, waiting tables, and working at a roller skating rink and a car wash.

Each of these jobs paid minimum wage, which at that time was $1.10 per hour.

He lied about his age to get a job in a box factory, and made slightly above minimum wage.

He was paralyzed from his waist down as a result of a fall down a flight of steps when he came home drunk one night. His doctor, priest, and parents told him he'd never walk again.

When he was eighteen, a former high school counselor (the same one who threw him out of high school the last time) asked him what his goal in life was. He responded that it was to get a part-time job, along with his full-time job, so he could earn more money. His goal in life was to work twelve hours a day at two poor-paying jobs!

He had such low self-esteem that his girlfriend threatened to quit dating him if he didn't quit feeling sorry for himself. One night, while on a date, she said, "Stop the car. If you don't promise to quit putting yourself down, I am getting out of this car and walking home."

If I asked you to describe this fellow, your first description of him would most likely be "loser!" If I were then to ask you what the chances were of this guy ever becoming a success, you would probably say "slim to grim." After all, you could cite any one (or all) of the following reasons why he couldn't become a success.

He was:

1. Born on the wrong side of town.
2. From a poor and dysfunctional family.
3. A high school dropout.
4. A gang member.
5. A troublemaker by reputation.
6. Full of too many bad habits—stealing, smoking, drinking, and fighting.
7. In poor health—skinny, hard of hearing, paralyzed.
8. Stuck in a dead end job.
9. Lacking goals.
10. Terribly short of self-esteem.

Quite frankly, "slim to grim" wouldn't be a bad answer. After all, he was poor white trash, born on the wrong side of town, a troublemaker, a high school dropout, a gang member, a physical wreck, and an all-around loser.

Now, let me introduce you to another fellow.

He has been married to his childhood sweetheart for thirty-one years and has two wonderfully smart, healthy, pretty daughters.

He is a college graduate as well as a law school graduate. He successfully practiced law for five years before he decided to become an entrepreneur and start his own business.

He founded several different businesses in industries including real estate, oil and gas, manufacturing, and finance.

He started—from his kitchen table—with an initial start-up loan of thirteen thousand dollars and ended up with a company that produced annual revenues in excess of $1 billion and annual earnings of more than $180 million.

He started and ran a company that revolutionized an entire industry.

Over the course of his business career, his companies created more than 10,000 jobs in the United States and internationally.

One year, his take-home salary (including dividends from his privately held company) exceeded $100 million.

He created and pioneered new financial instruments being used today on Wall Street.

He negotiated and concluded over $3.1 billion in Wall Street financial transactions.

His company was ranked in *Inc.* magazine's 500 Fastest-Growing Companies in America—four years in a row.

His list of awards includes:

- The American Academy of Achievement's Golden Plate Award. This award has previously been bestowed upon five U.S. presidents and three Nobel Prize winners.

- The National Entrepreneur of the Year Award by Merrill-Lynch, Ernst & Young, NASDAQ, *USA Today*, and *Inc.* magazine.

- *Business Week* magazine's award for "One of the Top 30 Family-Friendly Companies in America."

- The U.S. Chamber of Commerce—Blue Chip Enterprise Award.

- The Association of Southern Governors—Governor's Cup Award.

- The Better Business Bureau's "Torch Award" for ethics in the marketplace.

He has been included in *Forbes* magazine's list of the 400 wealthiest people in America. One magazine ranked him number twenty-five.

He has been inducted into the "National Entrepreneur of the Year" Hall of Fame.

He has been named as one of the top one hundred entrepreneurs of the last one hundred years.

He has been granted a permanent place in the Smithsonian Institute's Museum of American History for his "Visionary Use of Information Technology Which Produces Positive Social, Economic, and Educational Change."

Harvard Business School has written a case study based on him and his management techniques.

Seven different authors have used him as the subject of their books.

His management techniques are published in textbooks used in colleges and universities across America.

He and his wife live in a 12,000 square foot $2 million home.

He has had personal jets and secret service contingents at his disposal twenty-four hours a day.

He has donated millions of dollars to charitable organizations.

He and his wife gave each one of their eleven family members a gift of $100,000 because they wanted to share their good fortune.

He is happy and healthy and thinks he can accomplish anything he sets his mind to.

If I asked you to describe the second person, you probably would call him a "winner." After all, he succeeded at a large number of different challenges, and he continues to succeed. He is optimistic, positive, and eagerly awaiting the challenges and rewards to come from the next successful venture. He has a terrific family, a solid financial base, a wonderful life, and untold opportunities awaiting him in the future.

Most people would think that there is a world of difference between these two people. In reality, the only difference between them was a state of mind. The first fellow acted like a loser because he thought he was a loser. The second fellow became a winner because he believed he was a winner. I can make this statement with a great deal of certainty and conviction because both of these people I've just described are really the same person—ME.

The sole purpose of sharing this private piece of my life is to convince you that no matter what handicap you think you have, whatever you think is keeping you from achieving a more satisfying life, you can overcome that handicap and accomplish any goal you set for yourself.

Go back to the description of the first fellow and compare your life as it is right now to his. Be honest with yourself when you ask the question,

"Would I be willing to trade places with him?" Most of you wouldn't want to change places with him. If fellow number one could become fellow number two, in spite of all those handicaps, just by following the principles set forth in this book, just imagine what you will be able to do!

Introduction

The price of success is much lower than the price of failure.

—Thomas Watson

Shallow men believe in luck; strong men believe in cause and effect.

—Emerson

If you keep believing what you've been believing, then you'll keep achieving what you've been achieving.

—Mark Victor Hansen

The definition of insanity is to do the same thing you have always done, and expect a different result.

—Anonymous

In life, you don't get what you deserve; you get what you believe, plan, and expect.

—Bill Bartmann

If you could see what I see when I look at you, you would see a person who is smart, strong, dedicated, loyal, caring, and most importantly, capable of accomplishing any goal you set for yourself. I see a person with the power and talents to do anything you set your mind to. This power is within you and always has been within you. You doubt you have this power because you don't recognize it. Believe it or not, this is perfectly normal. Ninety-nine percent of the people in the world doubt their own abilities. That is why almost every major accomplishment in history has been made by the other 1 percent. By following the principles set forth in this book, you will become one of those in the top 1 percent.

The strongest, most powerful force in the world is the power of self-belief. From this power, all other things flow. Every invention, creation, and thing of utility known to humanity was spawned by a belief in the mind of the people who accepted the concept that they could actually create or cause things to happen. If they did not have this belief, they would not have the ability to withstand the frustrations that are always a part of this process. Without belief, they would have succumbed to the jeers and doubts of others as they progressed on the road to completion.

Alexander the Great believed he could conquer the world.

Christopher Columbus believed he could find a new passage to India.

Wilbur and Orville Wright believed they could fly.

Abraham Lincoln believed he could be president of the United States.

Henry Ford believed he could create the largest company in the world.

Ray Kroc believed he could sell billions of hamburgers.

Billy Graham believed he could create a global ministry.

Bill Gates believed he could become the richest man in the world.

(Your name)_____ believed (he/she) could_____.

Although the list is endless, every person who has succeeded (by whatever definition society happens to be using during that period) BELIEVED his or her goal was certain to be accomplished. This self-belief was so strong that no amount of adversity or frustration could stop her from continuing her quest. No setback, no matter how devastating, stopped him from believing that he was going to accomplish his goals.

The previous list of achievers was chosen because these people were not taller, smarter, better looking, younger, or in any other respect (save one) different than you or the rest of the people on earth. That one respect was their total, unrestricted belief in themselves. They did not think that they "might" succeed or "maybe" they would succeed or "if" something happened then they would succeed; they absolutely believed they were going to succeed. This belief was so strong that they conducted their daily life as if success were a certainty. For them it was only a matter of time. Even when they didn't know how, they still always knew they would.

Self-Belief: Our Views of Ourselves

Self-belief (or self-esteem) is the internal image our subconscious mind has of itself as it relates to how we feel about our personal capabilities to accomplish certain tasks. This image can be either positive or negative—or a combination of both—depending upon the task we are examining. It is an image created—and held firmly in place—by the information our subconscious mind receives when it inquires within. This image may or may not be accurate, and it may or may not be shared by anyone else in the world. It doesn't matter that the image of self as held by our subconscious mind may be inaccurate, or that it may (or may not) be consistent with the view others have of us as individuals. It is our belief, and that makes it the only one that counts. As a rational human, all our actions will be consistent with our own self-belief. It is virtually impossible for anyone to consciously act in a fashion inconsistent with his or her self-belief. We easily accomplish those things that we believe at the outset we can accomplish (positive self-belief), and rarely (if ever) accomplish things that we don't think we can achieve (negative self-belief). Therefore, to become a success, we must find a way to strengthen our existing positive self-beliefs while creating new ones. At the same time, we must find a way to weaken or reduce the negative self-beliefs we possess, while making sure we don't acquire any additional ones.

Self-belief is deeply rooted in the mind because it is tightly connected to our inherent survival instinct—self-preservation.

The self-preservation instinct is the strongest drive found in all living things. This instinct causes all living things to act in a manner consistent with self-survival and, at the same time, to avoid all things perceived to be harmful. Self-survival is more than just the avoidance of those things that might actually be fatal. It is also a perpetual movement toward things that produce pleasure and a movement away from things that cause pain. This pain may be other than just physical. It can also be mental or emotional pain, such as that caused by embarrassment or humiliation.

Self-survival in plants can be seen in the example of a houseplant: placed in the shade, it will distort its natural shape to grow toward sunlight.

In animals, the survival instinct is most often seen in the tendency to flee from any change in the environment, such as an unusual noise or smell. Anyone who has spent time in the outdoors has experienced an animal fleeing the scene if it hears a strange noise or picks up an unfamiliar scent. The deer may not know specifically what created the noise or caused the scent, nor does it know that it was caused by something that would in fact not be harmful to it. Its survival instinct is so strong that it doesn't care; it just flees. Biologists have confirmed in countless studies that fleeing at a sign of danger is a natural instinct as well as a learned instinct (or thought process).

In humans, we see this phenomenon demonstrated in our inability to do things to our body that the mind perceives as harmful. If you doubt this, punch a pillow as hard as you can. Now, attempt to strike yourself in the face with the same force that hit the pillow. You simply cannot do it! Your subconscious mind recognizes the harm this would cause, and it tells the muscles involved not to cooperate in spite of your conscious mind's command to the contrary. Your conscious mind is saying "do it," yet your subconscious mind is overruling the conscious mind. It is almost enough to make you wonder: **Just who is in charge . . . me (my conscious mind) or my subconscious mind?** Your subconscious mind exercises much more control over your activities than you ever would have guessed.

Our self-preservation instinct has only one mission: to protect and preserve the life support system within which it is housed—our mental and physical being. Much like a symbiotic plant or animal that attaches itself to a "host" and then depends entirely on that host for life itself, our self-preservation instinct is concerned primarily with the health and well-being of the "host." If the host ceased to exist, the guest would also cease to exist. Our self-preservation is not a separate organism attached to our thought process. Rather, it is part of this thing each of us refers to when we say "me" or "I." This is why it is called "self" preservation. It is an integral part of this thing we know as self.

Self-preservation is easily recognized when it is performing its function in a traumatic situation, such as jerking our hand away from a hot object or reflexively jumping away from a startling noise. It is less noticeable when it is performing an even more important function. This more important function is the inquiry it makes as to our internal opinion of whether we believe we are capable of performing a particular task.

Our self-preservation will not, I repeat WILL NOT, let us do anything it perceives as harmful (pain) to us. Failure—and the corresponding feeling of embarrassment, anxiety, or humiliation—is viewed as harmful to us. On the other hand, it will allow, and even help, us to achieve things beneficial to us (pleasure). The self-preservation's decision to impede us (or to help us) is determined by our self-belief. If our positive self-belief is high concerning a particular task, our self-preservation receives a signal indicating we are comfortable with our ability to perform this task. Therefore, there is little or no likelihood of failure. Self-preservation then views the proposed task as one it should assist in its desire to take us toward pleasure. If, on the other hand, our self-belief is low in regard to a particular task, our self-preservation receives a signal indicating that we are not comfortable with our ability to perform this task. Therefore, there is a high likelihood of failure. Self-preservation then views the proposed task as one it should impede in its desire to take us away from pain or failure.

Remember, self-preservation's job is to preserve us, meaning that all of its actions will be designed to take us toward pleasure and away from pain. While it might be argued that movement toward pleasure is (generally speaking) traveling in the same direction as movement away from pain, our self-preservation instinct views them as two entirely different functions. It looks to the amount of risk involved versus the amount of reward that might be obtained. In performing its analysis, it does not treat these two concepts as equal. It is both subjective and conservative; therefore, it gives a greater emphasis to items containing risk than it does items containing reward. Like a conservative banker, our self-preservation instinct thinks it better to forego potential reward than to take a potential risk. Like the over-protective parent trying to shield his or her child, it decides that if it foregoes a potential reward, the status quo has at least been maintained, and although the reward did not occur, we are still okay. If, however, it allows us to proceed toward an objective that contains risk, we can be exposed to some danger or pain. If this were to occur, we might suffer.

Our self-preservation views the embarrassment, anxiety, or humiliation of failure as pain. Its mission is to avoid pain; therefore, it will try to avoid failure in the most certain way possible. The most certain way possible to avoid failure is to not try anything of which you are uncertain. Our self-preservation analyzes all of the stored information available to it to determine whether we have data supporting the belief that we can accomplish this task. If it finds data supporting the conclusion that we can accomplish the task, it will help us achieve the objective. If it finds data that causes it to believe we will be unsuccessful in our attempt, its job becomes to deter us from trying to do this thing. One method it uses to deter us from doing something it feels will be harmful to us is to rationalize us out of our decision.

If self-preservation can rationalize us out of trying, it can guarantee we will not fail. This rationalization may take the form of sour grapes: "That goal wasn't worth having anyway," "The grass is always greener," or "I really would rather have something else instead." As this rationalization process begins, the excuses why we "didn't want," "don't need," or "will do it later" grow larger and larger. Pretty soon we are convinced that we didn't fail, we just decided not to pursue this silly goal. Or we convince ourselves that the rules weren't fair or that someone else got lucky. The list of tricks our self-preservation can use to deter us is limited only by our own imagination; therefore, it is virtually endless.

If our self-preservation instinct looks to our self-belief before it decides whether it is going to help or hinder, how can we ensure it will make the decision that will help us accomplish our goal? The answer is simple: we need to make sure that when the question is asked of our self-belief, that the answer comes back YES! The answer that comes back in response to the question is the answer stored in our memory bank. If this stored information is negative or uncertain, then the answer that comes back has to be negative or uncertain. If the stored information is positive, then the answer will come back positive. We can control the answer that will be produced by controlling the stored information available.

Another example in humans is the bodily change that immediately and automatically occurs (without our conscious mind even being aware of them) when we experience fear or danger. Our stomach quits digesting food, our heart begins to pump much faster than normal, and our adrenal glands begin to secrete adrenalin into our system. All of these things occur simultaneously and instantaneously to give our body the extra assistance it needs to respond to whatever frightened us. Adrenaline has been referred to as our "fight" or "flight" drug. There are numerous examples of superhuman feats performed by people under the severe stress caused by fear of imminent danger. Newspapers frequently print stories of these occurrences, such as a mother lifting the front of an automobile to free her trapped child, or a person effortlessly carrying someone twice his own weight from a burning building, or a blazing wreck prior to the vehicle blowing up. These feats have generally been attributed to the presence of adrenaline in the system. I would submit that while adrenaline helps, these feats are really just examples of how we are able to perform (as we are truly physically capable) when not being held back by our overprotective subconscious mind's fear that we might hurt ourselves. In this regard, our subconscious mind acts similarly to the overprotective parent who won't let her child engage in normal childhood activities out of fear the child might get injured.

Let me give you an example of how our self-belief and self-preservation can influence an outcome. When I was a freshman in high school, I wrestled at the ninety-eight-pound weight level. As part of the wrestling practice workout, the coach wanted all of us to do weight lifting exercises. Each session involved doing a number of standard lifts, including one called the bench press. In this exercise, you lie on your back on a bench, lower the weight lifting bar to your chest, and then push the weight upward by extending your arms. I had done this particular exercise with 125 pounds of weight countless times during the wrestling season. Each time I tried to go the next weight level of 130 pounds, I would fail and be unable to perform the exercise. My mind became accustomed to the fact that my limitation was 125 pounds. Every time I tried a heavier weight, I was unable to lift it.

One day as I was finishing my warm up workout at a lower weight level, one of my wrestling buddies walked by as I was lying flat on the bench, and I asked him to put on some additional weights. I had been warming up with one hundred pounds of weight on the bar. I asked him to add an additional twenty-five pounds. While I was catching my breath and not paying attention, he deliberately put on fifty pounds instead of twenty-five pounds. When he told me the weights were properly on, I began my lift. I performed it smoothly and flawlessly even though it was twenty-five pounds heavier than I had ever previously lifted!

Where did the extra strength come from? It was there all the time. My mind had become conditioned to my weight limitation and was impeding me from lifting anything heavier. Once my mind was deceived—thinking there were only 125 pounds on the bar, when in fact there were really

150—it allowed me to lift it.

Perhaps karate students demonstrate the classic example of this. Both our conscious and subconscious mind know it is really, really stupid to punch our hand into a stack of bricks. Our conscious and subconscious mind know that bricks are very hard and that if we were to do so, most certainly we would hurt or even break the bones in our hand. Yet students of karate do this as a regular exercise and do not hurt their hands—nor do they break bones. How is this possible? Very simply, karate students are taught how to convince the conscious mind that the feat can be accomplished, and they learn how to trick the subconscious mind into believing they are capable of doing it.

The karate student's conscious mind becomes convinced that the feat can be accomplished as he watches his instructor and fellow classmates accomplish the feat time and time again. But much like my weight lifting example, although the conscious mind is convinced that it is the brick that will break and not the hand, the subconscious mind is more concerned with the survival of the human body it is housed in, and it doesn't want that human body to get hurt. The karate student must trick the subconscious mind to allow the conscious mind to perform the feat. This is done by a series of hand and knuckle toughening exercises whereby the student punches a bowl of flour. The conscious and unconscious mind doesn't have any problem with that—even an overly protective unconscious mind doesn't envision any harm coming to the hand by punching into a bowl of flour. The purpose of the exercise is to toughen the skin of the knuckle so that when the fist is later used to punch harder objects, the skin will have become calloused and tougher. After several weeks of punching flour, the student graduates to punching a bowl of sand. Again, the subconscious mind is not afraid of the hand being punched into a bowl of sand. This too has the effect of toughening up the skin and knuckle. Soon, the student moves on to punching a bowl of raw rice. And again, the subconscious mind is okay with this. After several weeks of progressing through these and other punching practice exercises, the student begins to punch a stationary cocoa mat pad attached to the wall. The purpose of this exercise is to allow the student to begin hitting something hard, all the while further conditioning his hand and muscles for the brick-breaking feat he will someday be requested to perform. The next step in the training process is to allow the student to begin breaking boards. The boards themselves are made of white pine, which is relatively brittle and tends to break rather easily. The standard boards are generally twelve inches square and one inch thick. For the first few lessons, wider boards (which break even easier) and thinner boards (usually a half-inch) are used. This allows the student to succeed each time he attempts to break a board with his fist.

As the student gains confidence in his conscious and subconscious mind, the thickness of the board increases up to the one-inch level. Once the student is able to punch through a one-inch board with no difficulty, a second board is added. Over a period of several weeks, the student will progressively add more boards and will succeed each time he attempts to break them with a punch. Once the student is capable of punching through six one-inch boards simultaneously, he is ready to attempt breaking a brick.

Because the instructor wants the student to be successful during the first few brick-breaking exercises, he will do the same thing he did when the student began breaking boards. He will use less-than-standard-sized bricks. The bricks that will be used for the first few breaks are more brittle and of slightly thinner composition, so they will break easier. Once the student has mastered the thinner bricks, he will be allowed to move on to the standard-sized bricks.

This journey from punching into a bowl of flour all the way to punching a fist through a standard brick could take anywhere from four to six months. At each practice session, skin-and knuckle-toughening exercises are performed, along with the slow progression of breaking successively harder, thicker objects. All the while this process is going on, the student is observing his instructor and his fellow classmates doing the same or more difficult exercises.

The combined effect of this slow and methodical progression, along with an environment of camaraderie with others who share common goals, has convinced both the conscious and the subconscious mind that this student can punch his fist through a brick and remain unharmed.

All the physical exercise I described was an elaborate hoax to fool the subconscious mind into allowing the body to do what the body always had the capacity to perform. The student didn't get much (if any) stronger or faster during the intervening four to six months of this journey. All of the conditioning to the hand and knuckles really didn't have anything to do with the ability to break the brick. It may have had something to do with the fist not being bruised or sore after the event, but the conditioning of the skin—created by punching the flour, then the sand, then the board, and finally the small bricks—didn't make the brick break.

What made the brick break was convincing the subconscious mind not to interfere. In order to break the brick, the student needed to hit the brick with a fast and solid blow with the conviction that the brick was going to break. Physically, the student was able to do this on day one. Mentally, his subconscious mind would no more allow that than the subconscious mind would allow to punch himself in the face. But once the subconscious mind was lulled into believing that it would be the brick—not the hand—that would break, the subconscious mind didn't restrain the student when the student needed to punch fast and hard. Amazing, isn't it?

This survival instinct is so strong and so pervasive that it is automatically factored into essentially every decision we make. Each action we perform—whether physical in the sense of our mind telling our body to perform a certain task or mental as when our mind tells our conscious mind to perform a thought process—is instantly subjected to this automatic test: "Will the requested action do harm and therefore be inconsistent with self-survival?" This mind process happens so quickly and so naturally that we are not even aware that it is being performed. If we are to have any say-so in our own destiny, we need to learn how to control this process rather than let this process control us.

KEY POINTS

1. Every major accomplishment in the world has been made by the 1 percent of the people who strongly believe in themselves and in their abilities to accomplish a particular challenge.

2. Self-belief is the view our subconscious mind has of us.

3. Our self-belief may be positive or negative.

4. Our actions will always be consistent with our internal self-belief.

5. The strength or weakness of our self-belief will determine the likelihood of our success or failure as we embark on any action.

6. Self-belief is tightly connected to our inherent survival instinct—self-preservation.

7. Because self-belief is so strongly connected to self-preservation, it is first concerned with protecting us from harm or embarrassment.

8. Our self-belief will only allow us to do that which it thinks we can do safely.

9. Like a "conservative banker" or an "overprotective parent," self-belief is more concerned with avoiding risk than it is with reaping rewards.

Chapter One

UNDERSTANDING THE PROCESS

You will never rise above the image you have of yourself in your own mind.

—Joel Osteen

What you believe about you impacts you more than what others believe about you.

—Bill Bartmann

If one advances confidently in the direction of his dreams, and endeavors to live the life which he has imagined, he will meet with a success unexpected in common hours. He will pass an invisible boundary; new, universal, and more liberal laws will begin to establish themselves around and within him . . . and he will live with the license of a higher order of beings.

—Henry David Thoreau

The greatest discovery of my generation is that human beings can alter their lives by altering their attitudes of mind.

—William James

Your mind and a computer have one thing in common: neither of them know the difference between the truth . . . and what you tell it.

—Ken Blanchard

For as he thinketh in his heart, so is he.

—Proverbs 23:7

1

To control our future, we must first understand how self-beliefs—both positive and negative—are formed. It is my assertion that a clear understanding of how the process works is crucial if we are to make it work for us rather than against us.

I have read hundreds—if not thousands—of books on the power of positive thinking and self-motivation. These books (generally speaking) are very good at psyching us up and motivating us. However, after a short period of time, usually our enthusiasm begins to fade, right along with our faith in that particular author's method. This fading is a direct result of our not understanding the process itself. Each of these authors tells us the theory works. Next, they cite a number of examples to convince us the theory works. Then they lay out a number of steps we should follow if we want to succeed. This type of instruction is valuable and will work for a short period of time. The flaw in this method, however, is that it does not tell us HOW this process works. Our human nature is such that most (if not all) of us have difficulty accepting or believing something we don't understand. With the exception of perhaps certain religions where we accept something as true based on faith alone, most of us need to understand the fundamentals of a process and be satisfied with the mechanics of the inner workings before we truly accept it. Humans are basically skeptical of anything they don't understand.

As if we are all from Missouri (the "Show Me" state), we are waiting for someone to "show us." While it is important to know that something works, it is even more important to know how it works. This is especially true in this situation, since we are the ones that are now expected to live our lives by this new program (or process). The difference between being satisfied that something works and knowing how to do it yourself is the difference between watching a magician performing his act, and your performing the magic act yourself. If we just want to see (and believe) that it works, it is enough for us to watch him perform his feats of magic. On the contrary, if we are to take the stage and perform these same magic tricks, we must understand how they were accomplished. When we watch the show, we see, believe, and know that the trick works; one could say that we now believe in magic. There is a substantial difference, however, in believing in magic and being able to perform it ourselves. If we are to shape our self-image, we must know how it works. We need to know how it got the way it is and what we can do to change it.

THE MIND: WHAT IT IS AND HOW IT WORKS

A pure definition of "mind" is difficult to formulate, as this term has been used many different ways throughout history. The different ways of referring to the mind began about the same time as humans became aware we had one. Terms like *brain, mind, intellect,* and *soul* have often been used interchangeably. The debate over this definition has raged among philosophers such as Aristotle, Plato, and Thomas Moore, and has included psychiatrists and psychologists from Freud to Jung. Even today, neurosurgeons debate with philosophers and theologians as to the most correct definition.

It is not the intent of this book to find an answer to this centuries-old problem but rather to explain to each reader how this amazing function of the mind is accomplished, regardless of the current definition. For our purposes, we will refer to the brain as *that biological mass of cells and nerves located within our cranium.* We will refer to the mind as *the thing (or process) that allows us to store memories and create thought.* While the mind may be located within the brain itself, it is not the brain. It is instead a process involving chemical and electrical responses affecting various parts of the brain, which then allows us to initiate and control our physical functions.

PRINCIPLE NUMBER ONE: SOURCES OF DATA

With the rare exception of those few individuals born with some type of birth defect, we are all equal at birth. We all come into this world with generally the same physical and mental characteristics. The presence or absence of a positive self-belief is *not* dictated by:

- Our parents' genetic contribution.

- The neighborhood or side of town on which we were born.

- The amount (or lack) of formal education.

- Our family's financial condition.

- The color of our skin.

- The particular religion in which we believe.

While it is much more comfortable to accept one of these kinds of reasons as an excuse to believe that people with a positive self-belief are different than you or me because of something we have no control over, this is simply not true! *Principle Number One* requires that we accept the fact that we really are all created equal and that each of us possess the same amount of self-belief as any other person. Once we accept this principle, we can begin to examine the process that occurs within us that allows this power to present itself in either a positive or a negative fashion.

If we all come into this world with generally the same physical and mental characteristics, then it is our perception of the things that occur thereafter that shapes and molds our beliefs as to what or who we are and, more importantly, what we think we are capable of doing. We must, therefore, examine these perceptions that shape our beliefs. Where do these perceptions come from? What do they consist of? Let's have a look.

These perceptions are an accumulation of everything recorded by our brains, from the moment of birth to the present instant. Some theories hold that our brain is even capable of recording sensory information received while a fetus. This collection of independent pieces of data is the total library of information the mind has at its disposal when called upon to formulate a decision. There is no other information available. It doesn't matter that someone else has more or less data than we do. It is our data bank and our data bank alone that supplies the information about us to us. These pieces of information or data fall into one of four major groups or categories: objective sensory data, subjective sensory data, internally generated data, and extrasensory data. Let's examine each one separately.

OBJECTIVE SENSORY DATA

Objective sensory data is the factual information we receive from our five senses: sight, smell, taste, touch, or hearing. Each time we experience one of these senses, our mind records the actual experience we are sensing without adding or subtracting anything from the thing being sensed. This recording is sent to the brain in the same condition as it is received.

As we walk through the park on a pleasant afternoon, our eyes, ears, and nose are busy gathering in all the sights, sounds, and smells one might encounter in a park. If during this stroll we observe a tree, and if there is nothing so unusual about the tree to cause us to think of it as different or unique, our mind will record this piece of data as a regular or generic "tree." It will not give this input any additional significance because we saw it "just as a tree."

Another example of objective sensory data is as follows: Imagine yourself at a well-attended party. As you enter the main room where the festivities are, you notice two people engaged in conversation. These two people are looking around the room and are laughing about something they have been discussing. This observation would be recorded as objective sensory data under the bland category of "two people having a good time at a party." There is no special significance to this observation. After all, people at a party are expected to talk and laugh.

SUBJECTIVE SENSORY DATA

Subjective sensory data is the information we receive from any one of our senses that has attached to it our opinion of or reaction to that particular sensory experience. If we are strolling through the park and see a tree that has been struck by lightning and its branches are twisted and bent, we see not only a tree but also something else. We see a tree that has been damaged by some powerful force. Our mind does not record this sensory experience as just a tree, but rather, it records it as an example of what lightning can do to a tree. It may also record it separately as a tree with a grotesque shape or a tree that now looks like something else. It associates something else to its view of it as a tree. It gives the "tree" data a new or second meaning that wasn't available with purely objective sensory data. Our mind did something subjective to the objective sensory data when it added a second association.

Now let's change one detail of our earlier observation of the two people at the party. As you enter the main room where the festivities are being conducted, you notice two people engaged in conversation. These two people are looking at you and are laughing about something they have been discussing. The only detail we changed is that rather than looking around the room, now they are looking at you. The significance of this small detail change will depend upon your reaction to it. If you had no reaction whatsoever, it would be (as before) recorded in your mind as objective sensory data: two people having a good time at a party. If instead, you did have a reaction to this change in detail, the observation would be recorded as subjective sensory data based on the reaction you associated with it. Imagine that this situation really did occur, and ask yourself the following questions:

- Would I wonder what they were talking about?

- Would I wonder why they were laughing?

- Would I become self-conscious of my appearance?

- Would I become convinced they were talking and laughing about me?

- Would I get mad at them for talking about and laughing at me?

- Would I want to go over to them and ask what was so funny?

- Would I want to leave the party?

- Would I quickly attempt to find someone I knew at this party in order to have someone to talk to?

- Would I feel awkward?

- Would I feel nervous?

- Would I begin to perspire?

If the answer to any of these questions is yes, then the changing of one little detail provoked an emotional reaction. This reaction could have ranged anywhere from mild to extreme. The mere fact that you associated any reaction to this observation will cause it to be recorded as subjective sensory data. It is still the same fact—namely two people at a party who are laughing—but now it takes on an entire new meaning to you.

INTERNALLY GENERATED DATA

The third type of data our mind records and processes is internally generated data. When our mind takes two separate and otherwise unrelated pieces of previously received information and joins them together, the process creates and records a new and different piece of information. We commonly refer to this process as *thinking*. When we are engaged in thinking, we are not using our external senses to gather information. Instead, we are using information previously gathered. We use as many of these separately gathered and previously stored pieces of information as is necessary to formulate this new thought. Once this thought has been created, it is recorded by the mind as a piece of new data. This piece of new data is recorded in the same way as data gathered from external sources is stored.

An example of this type of data is the phenomena referred to as the self-fulfilling prophecy principle.

The self-fulfilling prophecy principle tells us:

> I am not what I think I am,
>
> nor am I what you think I am,
>
> but rather I am what I think you think I am.

When you think of yourself in terms of certain personal attributes or talents, your subconscious brain registers these thoughts and gives them a relative degree of significance.

When someone else thinks of you in regard to these same attributes or talents, your brain is not involved and, therefore, registers nothing—consciously or subconsciously. Your brain is not even aware of what someone else's brain is thinking.

When you believe someone else has positive or negative thoughts about your attributes or talents, your subconscious brain registers these thoughts, along with the emotional reaction you associated with this thought. This combination causes your subconscious brain to give this record a much greater significance than any prior information received.

Your perception of their thought about you creates a significant emotional reaction. Therefore, the thought you are having about what you think they think is being recorded in your priority information database as true . . . even if you are wrong!

These perceptions can be factually incorrect, and yet, if recorded in your brain along with the instructions to accept the proposition as true, your mind will accept them as true. It is easy to imagine the number of times this must have happened to all of us. We as humans build on our common experiences. This concept supports the truisms that the rich get richer and success breeds success. If we believe ourselves to be lucky, we act lucky, and we accept all neutral comments, looks, and other forms of communication as an affirmation of our belief that we are lucky; we ignore anything to the contrary. These affirmations are then recorded in our mind as the objective view that we think that an outsider thinks we are lucky. The next time we need support, we ask ourselves how we feel about being lucky, and our mind recalls this feeling and tells us that yes, we *are* lucky.

I have a vivid recollection of one incident in my life where I know the self-fulfilling prophecy principle worked in my favor. It occurred when I became aware that someone whom I respected as intelligent thought I was smart. When I learned she thought I was smarter than I had previously believed I was, I started becoming what I thought she thought I was.

After flunking out of law school, I needed a job. The only job I could find was at a ski resort in Galena, Illinois—approximately twenty miles from my hometown. The job was that of desk clerk at the hotel and ski lodge. To get the job, I had to go through a face-to-face interview with the hotel manager, John R. Counts. Mr. Counts was in his late fifties and was a seasoned veteran of the hotel industry. He had several academic degrees and a whole wall full of industry acknowledgements and awards. He presented a no-nonsense appearance and quickly let it be known that he would not tolerate second best at anything—or from anyone. I don't remember the specific questions he asked during the interview, but apparently, I must have given him satisfactory answers, as he hired me for the job.

Several weeks after I started my new job, Mr. Counts was transferred to a sister hotel in some other state. The new manager sent to replace Mr. Counts was Jennifer Swerdfeger. I got to work early, stayed late, and did my job as efficiently as I knew how. Although Ms. Swerdfeger and I did not become friends, we had a good working relationship. Her duties required her to spend a fair amount of time at the front desk where I was stationed. One day as I was performing a particular task, she walked by and said, "Good job, bright young man." I replied with something to the effect of, "Thanks for the compliment, but I am not sure I am a bright young man."

She turned and said, "Yes, you are. It says so in your personnel file." I had no clue what she was talking about and told her so. She asked me to follow her into her office. Once in her office, she opened up a locked file cabinet that contained all the personnel records. She said that after my interview with Mr. Counts he had made a handwritten comment in the margin of the interview form. She pulled out my file and handed it to me. In the margin, Mr. Counts had written "bright young man."

I had spent five and a half years in high school without graduating. I managed to muster a C average in college and had just flunked out of law school. All my academic life, I had been told I was dumb. In grade school, the nuns of St. Mary's stuck me in the corner for not following directions and for being a bad student. In high school, I had been suspended many, many times and finally expelled from both of the only two high schools in town. In college, I struggled just to get a C. My law school experience confirmed I was not very smart, let alone bright. Yet, here was a perfect stranger—a stranger with more academic and industry degrees than I had ever seen at that point in my life, and one who offered a sincere comment in the margin of a job interview form.

My first reaction was to dismiss it as some kind of joke or at least a mistake. But before I could even comment, Ms. Swerdferger beat me to the punch. She said, "You only worked with Mr. Counts for a couple of weeks before he was promoted and transferred, so you probably didn't get to know him very well." She went on to tell me that she had worked with Mr. Counts for more than twenty years—in this hotel and in others across the country. She then said, "Mr. Counts has earned the reputation he has because he is a good judge of character. His successes have been created by his ability to judge people. If he says you are a 'bright young man,' then, by God, you are a bright young man!"

His comments in the margin of an interview form—a form he never expected I would ever see—and the explanation offered by Ms. Swerdferger became a giant step in me reassessing my capabilities. True to the self-fulfilling prophecy principle, I started to become what I thought they thought I was.

EXTRASENSORY DATA

Something is said to be extrasensory if the recognition or awareness of it comes to us from something outside the five common senses of touch, taste, smell, sight, and hearing. Extrasensory perceptions have been called the sixth sense in recognition of studies that have been conducted and that continue to provide growing evidence of the existence of this form of information gathering. In recent years, we have learned that there are light spectrums beyond the range of our vision. We have also learned that there are sounds such as radio waves outside the range of human hearing. If we were to deny the existence of everything outside the range of perception of our five common senses, we would have to surrender many of the technological conveniences we enjoy today. This includes television, radio, cell phones, and our wi-fi connections. All of these devices transmit signals, pictures, and sounds in a manner that is imperceptible by any of our five common senses.

It is a basic law of physics that matter, once created, cannot be destroyed. Its chemical composition may be changed to such a degree that it may become something else, but it cannot be destroyed. An example of this phenomenon is water. In its liquid state, we recognize it as water. However, once we subject it to freezing temperature, it becomes what we recognize as ice. If we were then to subject it to extreme heat, it would first return to the state we call water, and eventually to the state we call steam or gas. As steam (or gas), water is essentially invisible to our five senses. Although we would no longer be able to readily identify the substance, this inability to identify it would not cause us to believe the steam ceased to exist.

When we think (or create) a thought, we recognize this thought as existing, even if we can't see or feel it. We know this thought is real even though it may be as difficult to identify as a radio wave or a color outside our light spectrum. It therefore follows that once a thought is created, it exists as an element of matter, even if it is not detectable by one of our common senses.

Extrasensory perception is based on the logical premise that a thought is an element of matter. This thought exists as such until it changes its composition. We are not concerned about what a thought becomes after it changes composition. We are only concerned about what a thought is and how it functions while it is still a thought. Assuming that we accept the proposition that a thought has physical properties and exists as an element of matter, what does it do? How does it act? Can it travel invisibly through the air like a radio wave, or is this thought that was created inside a human cranium forever trapped inside that particular skull? Quite to the contrary, scientific research has demonstrated that thought can be transmitted from one person to another across considerable distances. These studies have concluded that thought is no more trapped inside the cranium of the person who generated it than the sound of a radio is confined to the building that houses the radio station.

Principle Number Two: Priority Information

Some information in our memory bank has been given greater significance than other information.

Our brain is constantly receiving information. Every one of our senses is continually feeding new and additional information to our brain during each of our waking moments (and according to some theories, even while we sleep). Everything we hear, see, touch, taste, smell, or think is being recorded.

If the human brain had to sort through each of these millions and millions of pieces of information to make a decision, it would be a slow and cumbersome process. Instead, the subconscious mind will attach additional significance to certain pieces of information it deems more important than others, and it will first look to them when it is called upon to make a decision. This information that is most easily accessed is called priority information.

Visualize your mind as a giant storeroom where everything you have ever felt, heard, seen, sensed, or thought is located. As we begin life, this giant storeroom is a large empty chamber, capable of holding all the information we are going to encounter during our lifetime. Directly inside this giant storeroom is a row of file cabinets; the rest of this storeroom is completely empty. Now further visualize a file clerk standing at the entrance of this storeroom. It is this file clerk's job to see that every piece of information we receive gets placed in this storeroom. Each day, our senses provide millions and millions of pieces of information. The file clerk is required to put each one in this room. Our file clerk does not have the time or the ability to file each of these pieces of information in the file cabinets in a neat, alphabetized system for easy recall. There are simply too many pieces of information coming in all the time. The file clerk must differentiate between priority information and non-priority information. The clerk takes all of the non-priority information and throws it on the ever-growing pile in the center of the storeroom floor, and he files the important information in the file cabinets. This important information—the priority information—which has been neatly filed in the file cabinets, can be, and is, retrieved quickly and efficiently.

A visual that makes the file clerk's job a little more understandable is one of the skits from the old *I Love Lucy* show, starring Lucille Ball.

In one particular skit, Lucy had a job in a chocolate factory. Her job was to take pieces of chocolate off of a conveyor belt as they moved past her, and to wrap each piece of chocolate. She had been given instructions not to let any of the chocolates get past her workstation. While the conveyor belt is moving at a slow speed, she is able to keep pace with the chocolates coming down the conveyor belt, successfully getting each of them wrapped. As the conveyor belt begins to speed up, she is no longer able to keep pace, and she begins to stuff every fourth chocolate in her pocket while wrapping the other three. When the conveyor speeds up even faster, she begins to wrap every other piece while stuffing the other one in her work uniform pocket. As the conveyor speeds up again, she is unable to wrap any of them, and she starts stuffing them in her dress, her pockets, and her mouth.

The point is obvious—the faster the conveyor belt moves, the less able Lucy is to follow the original instructions of wrapping all the chocolates. Because she is not able to keep pace with the flow coming at her, she does the best she can. She wraps as many as she can . . . and anything beyond that gets placed wherever she can put it.

Our file clerk is just as overwhelmed as Lucy was. A recent Harvard study showed that one edition of the *New York Times* newspaper contained more information than the average person living in the seventeenth century would come in contact with during the entire course of his or her life. Think about that just for a minute. Today, we receive more information in one day (from one newspaper) than our forefathers of only several hundred years ago would receive over the course of their entire lives. Now, we know our brains haven't evolved or changed much over such a short time frame as 300 years. How can our brain possibly absorb, retain, and retrieve all that data? And that's just from one newspaper! It does not take into account the additional data we receive daily from TV, radio, magazines, or the Internet.

So our file clerk responds the same way as Lucy did. As the flow of data overwhelms the file clerk, the clerk can only get a small portion of it in the right place—the file cabinet. All of the rest of it ends up in a pile in the center of the warehouse floor. Unlike Lucy, who randomly decided which chocolate she could wrap and which chocolate went in her pocket or mouth, the file clerk quickly differentiates between the priority information (data with emotional attachment) and all the other data that comes into our warehouse.

PRINCIPLE NUMBER THREE: DEGREE OF EMOTIONAL REACTION

Priority information is given a greater weight than all of the non-priority information stored in our memory. The file clerk differentiates all incoming information as either priority information or non-priority information based on just one factor. That factor is the amount or degree of emotional reaction consciously associated with the information as it was being received. If there is little or no emotional reaction associated with a piece of information, it is deemed to have little or no significance and, therefore, is given little or no priority. As the degree or amount of associated emotional reaction increases, so does the degree of prioritization given to it by the brain.

This process is a function of our evolution as a species. Whether one believes in creation or evolution as the beginning of mankind, I think we can all agree that modern-day humans have progressed (or evolved) since the days when we used to live in caves.

Scientists have determined that since our caveman days, the size and complexity of the human brain has increased. The intellectual needs of a caveman were exclusively devoted to food, clothing, and shelter—the basics of survival. His brain didn't need the complex wiring required to live and function in the twenty-first century. Scientists have further determined that the outer and top-most layers of our brain—the convoluted cerebral cortex we envision when we think of a human brain—has been added over the last few million years. Prior to that time, our ancestors used the rudiments of a brain consisting primarily of the brain stem (the central trunk of the brain which continues downward to form the spinal cord, and which includes the medulla, the pons, the midbrain, and the thalamus) and interestingly, the limbic lobe.

The limbic lobe includes a number of separate regions, including the amygdala and the hippocampus. The limbic system has been shown to involve itself primarily with processes associated with the emotional status of the body and memory. The amygdala is specifically involved in emotional experiences and reactions, particularly those associated with fear, anger, flight, and defense. And the hippocampus has been determined to be the center of memory.

So when we look at our caveman brain, we see that it wasn't nearly as complex as the brain of modern man. We also see it was equipped with what it needed to survive. Although our caveman forefathers had a smaller brain, it was mean and lean—and very functional—all by design. The challenges the caveman met on an average day frequently determined his life or death. Like the deer that jumps and runs when it hears a strange noise or smells a strange odor, the caveman also had to be quick to react to ever-present danger. The caveman lived in a hostile environment where he was as often the hunted as he was the hunter.

The caveman's brain, sitting directly on top of the brain stem, with a hippocampus (which recorded memory) and an amygdala (which recorded emotional reactions—particularly those associated with fear, anger, flight, and defense), gave him the tools to survive in his harsh and hostile environment. To survive, he needed to quickly differentiate between things that would harm him and things that would not.

It didn't take long for the caveman's brain to learn that things carrying with them any emotional reaction should be quickly and permanently recorded in his memory—so he could respond promptly if that situation ever arose again. His brain also learned that things not carrying with them any emotional attachment were less important and didn't need to be retrieved so quickly . . . if at all.

Although modern man's brain has evolved by adding several more regions and has grown in both size and complexity, it still has the very same hippocampus and amygdala sitting on top of the brain stem. Though we no longer need to worry about saber-toothed tigers and other strange beasts, our limbic lobe still functions the very same way as it did for the caveman; it records emotions and memories. Every time we experience something with any degree of emotional attachment, that item of information gets priority filing in our brain and is ready for instant retrieval.

Psychologists are in general agreement that there are eight basic emotions:

Anger	**Fear**
Joy	**Sadness**
Acceptance	**Disgust**
Surprise	**Interest (curiosity)**

All of the other things we may call emotions, such as love, grief, sorrow, and pride, are really combinations of these basic emotions.

These emotions can exist at various levels of intensity, ranging from weak to very strong. Each of us has experienced one or more (if not all) of these emotions at one time or another. From our experiences, we know that our body reacts differently during a highly emotional period. Although it is true of all of them, the most significant and therefore the ones most recognizable are the physical reactions we experience when we feel the emotions of fear or anger. Our blood pressure goes up, our heart rate increases, our digestion stops, and we may even begin to physically shake. The degree to which any or all of these physical things occur is directly proportional to the degree of emotion we are experiencing at the time.

These emotional feelings are strong enough to make our body react; therefore, it follows that these emotions are equally capable of making our mind react differently than it normally does.

When our mind senses our body's physical changes brought on by an emotional reaction, it gives the information being received during this time new and greater weight. The mind realizes that the situation that is occurring is different than normal; the information must be more significant. This is part of our self-survival instinct. If the mind is to give an appropriate instruction for future survival-type situations, it needs to store this information where it can be readily accessed.

This theory can be easily tested by each of us. Take a moment and think of the most embarrassing thing that ever happened to you. As this recollection comes to mind, you will be able to vividly recall where you were, who was present, what was said or done by someone else, how you responded, and how you felt. The entire situation will appear in your mind as if it were an instant replay on television. This little exercise will convince you that your mind does not forget anything it records. Now try to think of the day thirty days after this embarrassing event. Can you recall what day of the week it would have been? What you did that day? Who you spent it with? Can you recall anything at all about that day? Most likely you will be unable to recall anything about the day thirty days more recent in your mind (that is of course, assuming nothing with emotional attachment occurred that day). How else can you explain why the brain chose to mark certain information for quick and accurate recall yet took more recent information that it gave little or no significance to and put it in our huge warehouse floor with mountains of other insignificant trivia? This latter information is available with total recall under the effects of hypnosis, so we know it is in there. Yet the brain did not deem the data important enough to mark for quick retrieval. The attachment of emotional significance was missing.

Many trial lawyers say juries are often convinced by confident testimony concerning traumatic events, believing that the memory must be accurate because the trauma left so deep an impression. The analogy prosecutors always use is, "Everyone remembers where he was on September 11, 2001."

Test the theory again. Try to recall something you know you experienced that would have little or no emotional significance attached to. It should be something that is a common occurrence—so common that you wouldn't associate any emotional significance to it. An example might be seeing the first robin in spring, looking at a full moon, starting an automobile, taking out the trash, or cutting the grass. Find something you know you have done or experienced a number of times. Now, try to recall exactly how many times you did this particular activity. Try to recall each one of these events individually. If you have chosen a common occurrence, you may be able to recall one or two of these incidents with a vague degree of specificity. But you will also know that you performed this act many other times and for some reason just can't seem to recall anything about it. Why did your brain give some of these mundane events greater recall priority than the others? Think about the ones you did recall, starting with the first one that came to mind. How or why was this one different from the rest? What happened, and what was said? Who was present? How did you feel? When you ask yourself these questions about the event you remember, you will find that this one was different than the rest in one way or another. Something happened that caused your brain to attach some degree of emotional attachment to this particular event.

PRINCIPLE NUMBER FOUR: SELECTIVE RECALL

The outcome or conclusion regarding the presence or absence of positive self-belief is dictated solely by the information our mind chooses to use when called upon to formulate an opinion about whether or not we believe we can accomplish a certain task.

Although the mind has access to every bit of information we have ever accumulated during our life, most of this information is lying in a huge pile in the middle of the warehouse floor. The great majority of the data we have stockpiled since birth came into the warehouse with little or no emotional attachment, and subsequently, our file clerk threw it on the large pile in the middle of the warehouse floor. Any attempt to extract a particular piece of historical data from this huge, disorganized pile would be like looking for a needle in a haystack. Besides, the subconscious mind already knows that there isn't much (if any) relevant information out there in the pile—or the clerk wouldn't have put it there in the first place.

When the subconscious mind wants to draw upon previously existing data to formulate an opinion regarding the task at hand, it looks exclusively in the file cabinets. The information previously filed in the file cabinets has already been determined by the clerk to be the only information that is important. The file cabinets contain only the information that came with some degree of emotional reaction attached.

Sadly for most of us, the majority of the information in our file cabinets—data that came in with some degree of emotional reaction attached—is negative information.

From our earliest childhood to the current time, we have been presented with negative reactions by others concerning our conduct or our activities. As a young baby, the most frequently heard word was **NO.** Our parents, in an effort to protect us, used this word whenever we were about to do anything they felt might injure us. This word is used so often, it is surprising that it isn't the child's first utterance, rather than the word "mom." From childhood on, we are constantly being confronted with negative associations.

Some direct ones are:

- "Don't do that."

- "Be careful."

- "You're so stupid."

- "Why do you do such dumb things?"

- "You'll never amount to anything."

Others of these are indirect, and perhaps not even meant for us to overhear:

- "She is not very pretty."

- "He is not as (good, fast, strong, smart, healthy, tall, handsome, qualified) as _____ is."

Yet others are indirect and come in the form of perceptions (correct or incorrect) that we accept:

- How do you feel when people quit talking when you enter a room?

- How do you feel when you notice someone pointing at you?

- How do you feel around people who were present when a superior criticized you?

Each of these negatives has been recorded with varying degrees of emotional significance. As such, each of the negatives that is relevant to the topic at hand is retrieved every time we ask ourselves whether or not we can accomplish a particular task.

All of our positive emotional reactions are also in the file cabinet and they too get reviewed. All of our prior successes, all of our victories, all of the times we managed to do well or "get it right" . . . these are also in the file cabinets.

Our subconscious mind will review all of them—the positive and the negative. It will weigh each of them according to the degree of emotional reaction attached to it. Those items with significant emotional attachment will be given more consideration than an item with less emotional attachment. If we have two conflicting pieces of data—one with a high degree of emotional attachment and one with a low degree of emotional attachment—our subconscious mind will decide in favor of the one with the highest degree of emotional attachment.

KEY POINTS

If we are to shape our self-image, we must understand how it got the way it is and what we can do to change it.

PRINCIPLE NUMBER ONE: SOURCES OF DATA

It is our perception of things that occur during our life that shapes and molds our self-belief.

Objective Sensory Data:	Factual information we receive directly from one of our five senses.
Subjective Sensory Data:	Information that we receive—from one of our five senses—that additionally has an opinion or reaction attached to the data.
Internally Generated Data:	Data created by our mind when it takes two pieces of data that already exist in the mind and combines them, making an entirely new piece of data. This is also known as a "thought."
Extrasensory Data:	Data that comes to our mind from a source other than one of our five senses.

These four methods produce all of the material stored in our brain. When our mind begins to search through all of our recorded information to determine whether we can accomplish the proposed task, it is only this information that supplies the raw material for the ultimate answer. The mind does not have any access to any other information. It can only look inward to data we have previously accumulated and stored.

PRINCIPLE NUMBER TWO: PRITORITY INFORMATION

All data that comes to our senses is stored in the warehouse of our mind. Some data has been given greater significance than other data. The data with the greater significance, "priority information," is stored for quick retrieval.

PRINCIPLE NUMBER THREE: DEGREE OF EMOTIONAL REACTION

The mind sorts out all incoming data as either "priority information" or "non-priority information," based on the presence or absence of an emotional reaction attached to the data.

The caveman brain was less evolved than is modern man's and it had two essential parts: the brain stem and the limbic system.

The function of the brain stem was to send messages throughout the body. The function of the limbic system was to record emotional reaction and memory. The only two functioning parts of the caveman's brain did the one thing that was most important to the caveman's survival—recorded things that had an associated emotional reaction into his memory for speedy retrieval so he could quickly recognize and avoid a similar event (danger) in the future.

Principle Number Four: Selective Recall

The mind does not use all of the data available to it when it makes a decision; rather, it uses only that information that it recorded as significant.

If our file cabinet is full of negative information, the message that comes back will also be negative.

Chapter Two

ALTERING THE PROCESS

If you believe, then all things are possible.

—Mark 9:23

One of the greatest discoveries a man makes, one of his great surprises, is to find he can do what he was afraid he couldn't do.

—Henry Ford

You can't think and act like a victim and expect victory.

—Bill Bartmann

No one can make you feel inferior without your consent.

—Eleanor Roosevelt

Things are not always as they appear.

—Mad Hatter to Alice

In chapter one, we learned the mechanical processes the mind uses to retrieve, record, and recall information:

- The mind receives information from our five common senses of sight, sound, touch, taste, and hearing. It also receives information from our internal representation (thoughts) and from our sixth sense of extrasensory perception.

- The mind records all the information it receives.

- The mind recognizes and treats emotional information as more significant than non-emotional information.

- Information associated with emotional significance is filed separately as priority information and, therefore, is retrieved faster and easier than all other information.

We also learned how self-belief is created. Self-belief is a product of the information we receive from our mind when we request information concerning our ability to accomplish a certain task.

Like an "overprotective parent," before self-belief allows us to attempt any action—any movement—our mind has to decide whether to allow us to complete the action or movement upon which we want to embark. Its decision will be consistent with ITS view of whether our attempt will put us at risk of harm (embarrassment, failure, humiliation, etc.).

The mind draws its conclusion as to whether we can accomplish this task from all available information to which it has attached emotional significance.

A positive self-belief occurs when the mind finds more positive emotionally significant information than negative emotionally significant information.

Conversely, a negative self-belief occurs when the mind finds more negative emotionally significant information than positive emotionally significant information.

We have also learned that our self-belief will almost always dictate whether we succeed or fail at an undertaking.

If our internal belief system (self-esteem) acknowledges that we can accomplish the task we are contemplating, the task is not only viewed as easy, but we also begin the task with a high degree of confidence—and successful completion is almost assured.

If our internal belief system (self-esteem) gives us negative feedback as to its opinion of our ability to accomplish the task, the task is viewed as difficult. We begin the task with a high degree of uncertainty and begin looking for excuses why the task wasn't important or why we shouldn't have to do it. The likelihood of successful completion is minimal at best.

Our human survival instinct is so strong that it will not let us do something it feels would be harmful (dangerous, embarrassing, humiliating).

Now that we know how the mind receives and records information and how this process affects our self-belief, we are capable of using this knowledge for our own benefit. We can now ensure that our mind receives and processes only that information that will facilitate our goals and make their accomplishment a virtual certainty.

As we will learn in this chapter, we can control and even manufacture the information sent to our brain. In this regard, it is crucial to understand that the mind does not concern itself with the truth of the data being recorded. Its job is not to weigh, analyze, or determine the logic or truth of a proposition. It is only to record the data in the file cabinet (if it has emotional attachment) or on the floor of the warehouse (if it does not).

This clear understanding of how the mind works creates several alternatives we can use to control the information that does get recorded (and ultimately retrieved) when that all-important question is being asked.

The most effective way to keep our mind from accessing negative information when it is called on for a value judgment is keep the number of negatives it has to call upon to a bare minimum. If a person were able to screen or exclude all negatives, the mind would not be able to find any when it began its search. Although it would be difficult (if not impossible) to exclude all negatives, we can take certain steps to reduce the number that get recorded. Remember, it is only the ones that get recorded and how they get recorded that impacts our self-belief.

1. Challenge the Data for Factual Accuracy

We not only have the right to be intellectually honest with ourselves, we have a duty to be honest. So often we automatically assume the worst interpretation is the most accurate interpretation. Additionally, we are quick to overgeneralize a negative. We should never make a bad situation worse than it really is, nor should we assume that just because someone said something hurtful about us that the statement is true.

When we perceive negative data about ourselves or our capabilities, we should challenge and screen it carefully to see if we concur with the factual accuracy of the data. If we can find anything about the data that is false or inaccurate, we should tell our mind to reject this data. The emotional reaction attached to the data won't matter if we have been successful persuading our mind that the data is not accurate. Remember, the mind itself will not question the validity once it is recorded.

Each time we have a negative thought about our capabilities, rather than accept this potential negative as a fact, we should ask ourselves:

- Is this really true?

- Is it true all the time?

- Have there ever been any incidents where it wasn't true?

- Then, we should remind ourselves of the time when it wasn't true.

Remember the example we used earlier about walking into a room where there was a party, and two people looked your way while laughing? If as in our previous example, you admitted this would have caused you to become uncomfortable, then you failed to "challenge the data for factual accuracy." Unless you were certain that they were laughing at you, you really had no basis to feel uncomfortable. Yet you did what most people would do—you made an assumption without bothering to determine the factual accuracy. Since you didn't bother to check the factual accuracy, you can never know whether they were laughing at you or something totally unrelated. Mathematically, your chances of being correct are 50 percent—but your likelihood of putting negative information in your file cabinet is 100 percent.

Think of what would have happened if you had made the opposite assumption and concluded that they were not laughing at you? Here again, that assumption has a 50 percent chance of being accurate—but has a 100 percent of NOT putting any negative information in your mental filing cabinet.

2. Defuse Negative Emotional Reaction

If we can't reject the negative data because it is inaccurate, we should at least attempt to defuse any negative emotional reaction attached to the negative. Negative data by itself won't hurt us. If the emotional reaction attached to the negative is effectively defused, the information will get recorded as objective sensory data with little or no emotional significance attached to it. As such, it will be stored on the pile in the middle of the warehouse floor and not in the file cabinet. If the information is in the pile on the floor, our mind is not going to access it the next time it inquires as to our capabilities.

The easiest way to defuse a negative emotional reaction is by analyzing the bias of the source and putting the negative statement in its proper perspective.

"Who made the statement?"

- Does he know what he is talking about?

- Does she have all the facts?

- What is his source of information?

- Was she present when the event occurred?

- Is he basing his opinion and his statement on scuttlebutt and rumor?

- Is she biased?

- Does he have his own agenda?

- Does her opinion of you conflict with your opinion of yourself? If so, who is the best qualified to formulate such an opinion?

    - Why would you ever let someone else's opinion of you trump your opinion of you?

    - Your opinion of you is the only one that matters!

Another effective way to defuse a negative is to put it in the proper context.

When we succeed, we know, recognize, and understand that our successes are never as important to someone else as they are to us. Sometimes we are even disappointed to know that our successes really don't matter that much to anyone else. We also know that even if others do become aware of our successes, their memories are relatively short.

So, when we succeed . . .

We acknowledge that most people never even become aware of our success.

And . . .

We acknowledge that our success wasn't very important to some people, and to others, it simply didn't matter at all.

And . . .

We acknowledge that even those who learned of our success tend to forget it very quickly.

Why then, when we fail, do we conclude just the opposite?

- We think our failure is widely known.

- We think our failure is very important to others.

- We think our failure matters to everyone.

- We think no one will ever forget our failure.

When we fail, we think the whole world is watching—that everybody knows we just failed!

Be honest—do you think they really know? Do you think they really care? Even if they know and do care, should their opinion control who and what we think we are? Are these people even qualified to formulate an opinion of you? Do they have all the information required to formulate an accurate assessment?

Your baggage really isn't as big or as bad to anyone else as it seems to you. We are all self-conscious of what we perceive others may be thinking about us. In reality, most of them are not thinking about us at all—and even if they are, should their opinions of us change our opinions of ourselves???

3. Don't Overgeneralize Negatives

If we can't challenge the factual accuracy of the statement and can't defuse the negative, then we must make sure we are not overgeneralizing a negative.

One of the common mistakes we make is to allow a specific failure or mistake to be radiated out into a blanket statement our mind hears, records, and accepts as universally true.

When frustration sets in (and it often will), be careful how you express your frustration. Remember, our mental file clerk doesn't know or care about the difference. The clerk's job isn't to evaluate, it is simply to file the data in the file cabinet or throw it on the warehouse floor.

It is during these periods of frustration with a specific problem that most people speak in general or universal terms. Although their frustration typically relates only to a unique or specific thing, the statement created during a moment of frustration may be stated as if applying universally.

For example, a golfer who misses with a putt may say, "I am the world's worst putter," "My putting game is terrible," or "I can't putt."

A student having trouble with her math homework may say, "I hate math," "I'm no good at math," or "I'm stupid."

A salesman who just found out he didn't get the sale he was expecting may say, "I just can't seem to close big deals," "I'm not a good salesman," or "No matter how hard I try, it just doesn't seem to work."

Every one of these comments is inaccurate, yet each one of them was recorded in the mind as if it were true. Remember, the mind does not verify the accuracy of any statement it receives. It merely records it for later retrieval (and the bad news is it will retrieve it the same way it was entered—as universals). Think of how difficult it will now be for the golfer to become a good putter. The next time he lines up a putt, he will subconsciously call upon his memory bank to give him assistance and confidence on the putt. Yet the information that will come to the surface will be, "I'm the world's worst putter," "My putting game is terrible," or "I can't putt." Care to make a wager on his ability to sink this putt?

Learn to make a concentrated effort to de-universalize any negative statement you might make (if you must make one at all). Rather than say, "I'm the world's worst putter," say, "That was a bad putt." By doing so, you will be able to vent your frustration without limiting your opportunity for future success.

If you must acknowledge negatives at all, keep them short and simple. Limit any negative statement to a very specific situation with an equally specific time frame. The more specifically you can limit this negative, the less applicable it will be to any problem your mind is searching for an answer to in the future. Change the sentence structure to make it a specific statement with a specific time frame, rather than a universal statement with no time constraints. For example, "I don't understand any of this," could become, "I am having trouble understanding this part of the problem."

Go back to the putting example: "I am the world's worst putter," could become, "I don't understand what I am doing wrong today . . . I am a better putter than this."

4. ATTEMPT TO BALANCE EVERY NEGATIVE WITH A POSITIVE

As I said earlier, we should be intellectually honest with ourselves. We shouldn't be in denial when negatives occur—and they will indeed occur. We shouldn't ignore the reality of what just happened. We should face our negatives squarely and honestly. This means that:

- After we have challenged the data and determined it is indeed factually accurate and a negative has occurred, and . . .

- After we have defused as much emotion as we can concerning this negative, and . . .

- After we make sure that we aren't overgeneralizing this negative and we have narrowed it as much as we can . . .

- Then we should admit that it happened!

At the same time that we admit this factually accurate, emotionally defused, narrowed negative, we should search our memory bank to find a positive of equal or greater size and emotion. We should admit the negative while reminding ourselves of the time we accomplished an equally large or larger positive of the same general category.

If the negative is the golf putt that didn't go in, think of the time when you drained one from the far side of the green.

If the negative is failing to make the big sale, think of the time when you did make a sale as big or even bigger than this one.

If the negative is having trouble with the math homework, think of the time when you did well on a math exam or received good marks for a math project.

If you can't find a positive that fits exactly, find the one that fits the best. The mere exercise of finding a balancing positive will cause your mind to give this negative very little consideration. You deliberately caused your mind to look for a positive when it otherwise would have been focused intently on the negative thing that just occurred. You had succeeded in steering the mind's attention away from a negative and toward a positive!

You effectively screened, defused, narrowed, and balanced a negative. You will now have one less negative in your file cabinet.

5. DON'T CREATE YOUR OWN NEGATIVES

During our lifetime, each of us has picked up a substantial number of negatives from others around us. These negatives may have come from our parents, teachers, co-workers, or even our friends. Amazingly, the greatest number of negatives stored in our memory bank came from—us.

Have you ever heard the statement, "Don't be so hard on yourself"? It is a statement that is more true than most people have ever realized. Every time you come down on yourself (regardless of the reason), you create a negative piece of data in your memory bank. The statement you made has been recorded in your mind the same way it would have been recorded if another person had made it. It carried with it the same feeling of conviction or degree of emotional reaction that you associated with the statement.

When we are having difficulty with a given project, it is easy to say, "I don't understand this," "I can't figure this out," or "I don't know how to solve this problem." These statements are accepted by the mind at face value. Then as we continue trying to solve this problem, our mind accesses this statement and reaffirms that we can't accomplish this task. Instead of our mind accessing useful, positive information that might have helped us with this dilemma, it accessed the conclusion that we are incapable of solving the problem. It now not only fails to provide the assistance we need, it makes the job all the more difficult. That which we let our mind accept as true, becomes true.

Remember what we learned earlier: it doesn't matter how our brain receives this information (even if it comes solely from us), because it will eventually believe whichever proposition it has the most evidence to support.

When I was eighteen years old, I worked in a meatpacking plant. One of my co-workers was Michael Donovan. I respected and looked up to Michael because he was going to college, and he was someone who I thought was a really smart guy. From time to time, Michael and I would have occasion to talk during smoke breaks or our lunch hour. One day as we were conversing, he stopped me in mid-sentence and said, "Why do you do that?" Not knowing what he was referring to, I asked him what he meant. He responded, "Every time you begin a conversation, you start with the words 'I'm sorry,' and then you follow with what should have been the first words out of your mouth." Michael went on to tell me in rather strong words, "You have nothing to be sorry about; don't ever apologize when you shouldn't." He then said, "Starting a conversation with words like 'I'm sorry' makes you just that—one sorry son-of-a-gun." When Michael told me that, I was dumbfounded. I had no idea that I was actually saying, "I'm sorry" at the beginning of each conversation. When I thought about it, I could recall that I had in fact used those words—but they were formulated subconsciously without me ever thinking about them or making a conscious decision to use them. Apparently, my subconscious mind had such a negative "sorry" perception of me that it wanted to make sure that perception was communicated to everyone with whom I spoke. By doing so, I lowered everyone's expectations of me. By lowering the expectation level, I now wouldn't be required to perform or function at the same standard as everyone else. My subconscious was helping me (and itself) survive by making the standard I had to achieve lower and easier to reach.

Now, I am sure my subconscious didn't do this because it wanted me to be lazy and to find the easy way out. Instead, I believe my subconscious had received so many messages of failed attempts that it truly believed I was not very competent—not capable of accomplishing much—and wanted to lower the standard so I would have a better chance of getting along in life.

Although immediately—from that moment on—I paid strict attention to how I started a conversation and made sure the words "I'm sorry" never fell from my lips (unless it was in the factual context of something for which indeed I was truly sorry), reprogramming my subconscious didn't happen with just one revelation.

My subconscious had been accumulating data for many years. The net import of the data it had accumulated had convinced my subconscious that I was indeed a sorry person. I wasn't going to be able to snap my fingers and make it change this opinion based on lots of separate data accumulated over a long period of time.

About one year later, I was driving Kathy (now my wife) back to her part-time job as a counselor at a Girl Scout camp. Today, forty years later, I can vividly remember the stretch of highway we were traveling on when she said a few words that changed my life.

As we drove down the highway engaged in conversation—I was complaining or moaning or doing some "woe is me" about something crappy that was happening in my life—and in the course of that discussion, I had made the comment, "Well, that's all a guy like me can hope for." Kathy came absolutely unglued. She slapped her hand on the dashboard of the passenger seat and in a very loud voice said, "Stop the car—I want out!" I had been dating this girl for most of five years and had never heard her raise her voice . . . and here she was slapping a dashboard and in a very loud voice, demanding to be let out on a lonely stretch of highway, in the middle of nowhere, in the dark of night. Even more shocking and surprising, I didn't even know why she had made such an utterance. I was not aware of anything I had said that should have—or could have—provoked such an outburst.

I was stupefied by her reaction. I didn't know what to do. Here was the lady I loved, acting really, really weird, out in the middle of nowhere. I quickly pulled the car over onto the shoulder of the highway. Once the car came to a stop, I looked at her in bewilderment and asked, "What just happened, and what is going on?"

Her words are still burned into my memory (talk about an emotional reaction making an easily retrieved impression). In a loud and animated voice, she said, "I am sick and tired of listening to you put yourself down. I love you, and I respect you for what you are, who you are, and what you can become. But you have such a low opinion of yourself that there are times when you make me sick!"

It was then that the words Michael Donovan had told me a year earlier took on a whole new meaning. I realized that Kathy was right—I was always putting myself down. Though I had quit using the words "I'm sorry," my internal belief system had not changed. My subconscious still believed I was not very competent, not very capable, and was basically still a sorry son-of-a gun. But the real revelation was that by my words and actions, I was continually and perpetually reinforcing that very opinion upon my subconscious mind. Every time I did the "woe is me" or the "gee, this is all I am supposed to do/get/have" routine, I was reinforcing and strengthening the negative opinion my subconscious mind had of me.

KEY POINTS:

1. A positive self-belief occurs when the mind finds more positive emotionally significant information than negative emotionally significant information.

2. Conversely, a negative self-belief occurs when the mind finds more negative emotionally significant information than positive emotionally-significant information.

3. Our human survival instinct is so strong that it will not let us do something it feels would be harmful (dangerous, embarrassing, humiliating) to us.

4. We have learned that our self-belief will almost always dictate in advance whether we will succeed or fail at an undertaking.

5. We can control and even manufacture the information sent to our brain.

6. The more negative information we can screen or exclude from our mind, the less it will have to deal with when it searches our mental file cabinet.

7. We should challenge any negative data input.

8. We should defuse any emotional reaction attached to the negative.

9. We should not overgeneralize negatives.

10. We should balance every negative with a positive.

11. We should make sure we are not creating our own negatives.

Chapter Three

IMPLEMENTING THE PROCESS

RULES OF THE ROAD

We are bound by nothing except belief.

—Ernest Holmes

Give me a stock clerk with a goal, and I will give you a man who will make history. Give me a man without a goal, and I will give you a stock clerk.

—J.C. Penney

The thing is to understand myself, to see what God really wishes me to do . . . to find the idea for which I can live and die.

—Soren Kierkegaard

Forgetting what lies behind and straining forward to what lies ahead, I press on to the goal.

—Philippians 3:13–14

In order to succeed—you don't always have to know "how," but you must always know "you will."

—Bill Bartmann

The ultimate purpose of learning how the mind works is to be able to use this knowledge to help us achieve those things that we deem important in our life.

Our individual goals will vary widely. Since each of us is a unique individual, it makes perfect sense that we would want different things. The principles in this book have helped thousands of people successfully reach their individual goals. I have listed a few of them just to show the diversity and to further demonstrate that these principles apply to EVERYONE who wants ANYTHING.

- A female office worker whose goal was to become a "stay-at-home mother."

- A teenage girl who wanted to become a high school cheerleader.

- A young girl who wanted to become a champion equestrian.

- A woman who wanted to travel to Calcutta to work with Mother Teresa.

- A teenage boy who wanted to purchase his first automobile.

- A lady who wanted to run her own business and become a millionaire.

- A college student who wanted to get accepted into graduate school.

- A young man who wanted to become a professional athlete.

- A single mother who wanted to purchase her own home.

- A young man who wanted a singing career.

- A corporate executive who wanted to switch careers.

- An elderly gentleman who wanted to relocate to be closer to his children.

- A young man who wanted to compete in the Olympics.

- A recent college graduate who wanted to switch professions.

- A married couple that wanted to improve their marriage.

- A salesman who wanted to earn a promotion.

- A young lady who wanted to start her own business.

- A man who wanted to write a "best seller."

- A businessman who wanted to work less—without reducing his income.

- A man who wanted to retire at age fifty.

So far we have learned the mechanical applications of how the mind either helps or hinders us in the pursuit of our goals. Now we will learn the rules that will allow us to achieve our individual target.

This two-step process of learning the mind's mechanical applications and then the rules that apply is similar to the two-step learning process you engaged in when you learned how to drive an automobile. Before you took your first drive, you had to learn the difference between the accelerator and the brake. You also had to learn when and why to shift the transmission. You had to learn how much to turn the steering wheel to get the result you really wanted. This first part of the driving process was mastering the mechanical applications.

The second and equally important part was learning the rules of the road. You had to learn which side of the road you were to drive on, how fast you could go, when to yield, when to stop, or when to just get the heck out of the way. Both the mechanical application and the rules of the road are of equal importance. It doesn't matter how well you understand the mechanics of an automobile or how practiced you are at driving one, if you do not understand the rules of the road and the difference between a green light and a red light, you will eventually end up in trouble. Likewise, it doesn't matter how well you know and understand the rules of the road; if you haven't learned the mechanical applications of how to stop a car when you and a train are both trying to use the same railroad crossing, you are not ready to drive.

You have already learned the first part of goal attainment: the mechanical application of how the mind receives, records, and recalls information. The second part concerns itself with the rules that will ensure success. As in the example of driving an automobile, both parts are equally important and necessary; knowledge of either one alone will not replace ignorance of the other.

Do you remember your first "drive"? That which we do so casually now sure was awkward and uncomfortable the first time we did it. Likewise, some of the things you have already learned and some of the things you are about to learn will seem equally awkward at first. Like driving an automobile, once you learn how and then practice your skills, it will become easier and easier until you finally take it for granted.

RULE #1

Make Sure It Is <u>Your</u> Goal That You Want to Achieve.

There are two sources of unhappiness in life.
One is not getting what you want; the other is getting it.

—George Bernard Shaw

I don't know the secret to success, but the key to failure is to try
to please everyone.

—Bill Cosby

The indispensable first step to getting the things you want out of life
is this: decide what you want.

—Ben Stein

Set your mind and keep it on the higher things.

—Ephesians 2:7

True success is achieving YOUR goal—not one set by someone else.

—Bill Bartmann

I have purposely made this Rule #1 because it is the most important rule of all.

Be honest with yourself. Make sure the thing you are about to say you want to accomplish is really what you want to accomplish. Don't set your objective to please someone else—set it to please you. Yes, it is nice to make others happy, and it is nice to do nice things for others. But when you are talking about your life's objective, the first person you need to be able to satisfy is yourself. As Shakespeare said: "To thine own self be true, and thou canst not then be false to any man." So many people go through life trying to make others happy and never end up achieving their own happiness. Your life and your existence is all you are and all you have—why give it away? Instead, achieve your objective—your life's promise—and *then* spend time, effort, money, or whatever is necessary to help those to whom you feel so obligated. Give them the things you reap from your success—don't give them your life.

We all know boys in little league who are there not because they want to be, but instead, they are there to make their dads happy. We all know little girls who take ballet lessons because they want to make their mothers happy. We know sons and daughters of businessmen, lawyers, and doctors who majored in business, law, and medicine in college and then pursued a business career, a legal career, or a medical career—to please one or both of their parents, even though they would have preferred doing something else with their lives. We all know women who work forty-plus hours a week— who would rather be home raising their children.

We only have one life to live. Why spend most of it pursuing something only to accomplish it and then find out we really didn't want it, or we really could have done something different? What a shame, and what a waste of the most valuable of all of your resources—your very existence!

No matter why you are where you are and no matter how you got there, now is the time for you to decide how you want to spend the rest of your life. As you read these words, you need to know that today may be the most important day of your life. Today may be the day you realize you have the power to change your life. Once you make your decision, you will have a target in sight, and these principles will help you achieve your objective.

As our now-grown daughters were going through their teenage years, Kathy and I worried about them like all parents worry about their teenage children. We worried about who they were hanging out with, what they were doing, and whether they would be in an environment with drugs, alcohol, and sex. We knew that we had given them (okay, I didn't contribute much—Kathy did all the heavy lifting of raising our daughters) the best guidance we were capable of giving. We also knew we had endeavored to make them aware of the consequences of risky and dangerous behavior. We hoped that we had taught them good common sense and had given them a strong moral compass. But even after thinking all of those things parents like to think, we knew once they left the house, they would make their own decisions for themselves by themselves. Each time they left the house to go to the mall, to go to someone else's house to study, or to go out on a date, we would see them off by saying two things: "We love you," and "Choose wisely."

That was our way of saying, "We love you unconditionally—no matter what you do—but we also respect you enough to know that you have the power to choose what you do, and we think you will always "choose wisely." We wanted them to know that the decisions they made would/could impact the rest of their lives.

I am happy to report that both of our daughters are now college graduates, and both are happily married and moving forward in their respective careers. We don't really know what happened all of those times they were supposed to be going to the mall, studying, or on a date—and perhaps someday they will share those stories with us—but we do know they did "choose wisely."

Why am I telling you this story? Very simply—because you, too, are about to make a choice, and I want you to "choose wisely." You aren't going to make a choice about smoking a cigarette, drinking a beer, or dating someone your parents aren't real crazy about. No, the choice you are about to make is much more important than any of those. The choice you are about to make will decide the rest of your life.

You are about to decide your life's goal. Make sure it is your goal and not someone else's. **CHOOSE WISELY.**

RULE #2:

Don't Label It a "Goal," Call It a Promise.

Great minds have purpose; others have wishes.

—Washington Irving

The poorest man is not he who is without a cent, but he who is without a dream.

—Pennsylvania School Journal

Always bear in mind that your own resolution to succeed is more important than any one other thing.

—Abraham Lincoln

You do not have because you do not ask.

—James 4:2

If you change your focus—you will change your life.

—Bill Bartmann

Most self-help books give you guidelines or suggestions on how to achieve a goal. I believe they have started you off on the wrong foot, and have created a predetermined situation in which it will be okay if you fail to achieve that thing you are calling your goal.

Think about how the word goal is used in our society. We describe a goal as a lofty ambition, something to shoot for, something to strive for, or something to work toward. All of those descriptions imply that your objective will be difficult to achieve—which carries with it an implied message that it is just as likely as not that the ultimate goal will not be achieved. By describing the thing we want as a goal, we have created a situation in which our mind already knows it will be difficult to accomplish, and, at least in most circumstances, okay (or at least forgivable) if we fail. Goals are like New Year's resolutions . . . frequently made and rarely accomplished.

Take a moment and think about all the goals you have set for yourself in the past. Also think about all of the goals you have ever heard that others have set for themselves. Once you have that picture in your mind, ask yourself how many of those goals—yours and others—were actually reached. The answer usually is "not very many." If that is true (and it always is), then think of what the word goal has come to mean to you. It has come to mean that a goal is something you should try hard to achieve because it would be fun or good to have, but most of the time, goals aren't really achieved.

If you start out believing (from experience) that most of the time when you try to do something it isn't going to work, how confident are you when you attempt to do it the next time? The honest answer is obvious—not very confident at all! You start out shooting for a goal, wanting to hit it but also knowing it probably isn't going to happen. The mere fact that you think there is a possibility it may not happen has already begun to condition you for failure. Now each of us may have answered the question, "How often do we fail to reach a goal?" with a different percentage answer. Some of us may have said we hit our goals 90 percent of the time (if you said a number anywhere near this high, you are one extraordinary human being, and you shouldn't be reading this book, you should be writing it). Others may have a much smaller number. Regardless of what percentage of the time you say you hit your goals, look at the reverse (or reciprocal) percentage. If you say you hit your goals 70 percent of the time, this means you failed 30 percent of the time. If you say you hit your goals 60 percent of the time, then you failed 40 percent of the time. Now how confident of success are you when you begin to do something where you previously failed 30 or 40 percent of the time in the past? Obviously, you would not begin this journey with a high degree of confidence in a successful completion.

Now take a moment and think about all the promises you have ever made to yourself or to someone else. Also think about all the promises you have ever heard others make. Once you have that picture in you mind, ask yourself the same question you asked a minute ago: "How many of those promises were met or kept?" If you have been honest with yourself as you did these two drills (and if you haven't, quit wasting your time reading any more of this book and go back to watching TV), you will have answered that the percentages of "promises kept" is much higher than your percentage of "goals achieved." Interesting observation, isn't it?

Why is this percentage so much higher—almost 100 percent—for just about everyone?

We keep our promises at such a high percentage for three distinct reasons:

1. Emotional Attachment

A promise carries with it a much deeper sense of responsibility to the person to whom it is made, whether that person is you or someone else. Because it carries this deep sense of responsibility, a promise carries with it emotional attachment. When you make a promise, your emotions are involved. You aren't just making idle chatter. You are serious, and you intend to do this thing you are now promising. Because of the emotional attachment, the file clerk in our mind will now give this promise an immediate priority filing in the filing cabinet.

When we make a promise, we have every intention of doing what it is we say we are going to do. We do not make promises we do not intend to keep. Promises don't carry with them (from day one) a built-in excuse for not delivering. They are really quite the opposite—they carry with them a responsibility to deliver that which has been promised.

2. History of Success

Our mind recognizes that we have a history of success when it comes to making promises. It knows we have historically achieved an exceptionally high success rate (near 100 percent). It therefore assumes (based on this history) that we can and will keep this promise. Rather than being preconditioned for failure (because of a history of failure), our mind is preconditioned for success (because of a history of success).

These prior successes carried with them a positive emotional attachment. When we did what we promised we would do, we "felt" good about ourselves. That warm buzz, that good feeling—that was an emotional reaction. Our file clerk recorded this data in our file cabinet as a positive emotional reaction.

3. Role Reversal of Our Subconsious Mind

Our subconscious mind switches from the role of "overprotective parent"—attempting to talk us out of our goal—to the role of the "helpful parent" who is going to clear the path and make it easier to succeed!

Think of the difference between setting a "goal" to quit smoking and "promising" someone you love (your spouse, your parents, your children) that you will quit smoking. In the first instance, if you decide to resume smoking, it is of little consequence to anyone but you that you failed to achieve this "goal." If, however, you have promised someone you love that you were going to quit and then later resumed smoking, you would be afraid or embarrassed to tell the person you previously promised that you failed to keep your promise.

If you fail to keep a promise made, you will suffer (experience) an emotional reaction: shame, embarrassment, or disappointment. Remember, our subconscious mind does not want us to fail or suffer the emotional pain of embarrassment or humiliation. So what does it do? It helps us keep our promise (self-survival). Instead of finding excuses why we can't, why we shouldn't, or why it is okay to give up on a goal, it does just the opposite: it helps us keep our promise because avoiding the emotional pain, embarrassment, and humiliation of breaking a promise is consistent with self-preservation.

The internal dynamics have just shifted 180 degrees. Our subconscious has one job and only one job, and that is self-preservation. Our subconscious defines self-preservation as keeping us away from pain, embarrassment, humiliation, and failure.

When we set a goal, our subconscious remains true to its mission by acting like an "overprotective parent" who is attempting to talk us out of taking any risk, for fear we might fail. If we have already set a goal and our mind can't stop us from setting the goal, it begins to give us reasons why it is okay to discontinue goal's pursuit and begins to give us reasons and excuses why this goal wasn't a "good utilization of our time."

When we set a promise, the opposite happens. Now, our subconscious keeps true to its mission by acting like a "helpful parent" and begins to help us accomplish what we have promised. The subconscious knows that if we fail to keep a promise, we will suffer pain, embarrassment, humiliation, and failure—and its job is to keep us from suffering those things.

By changing the way we think about the process, we have just increased our likelihood of success by a huge margin. We will still have some work to do, but now we are positioned for success. And most importantly, we now have our subconscious helping us achieve our objective.

Here is an example of the difference between *setting a goal* and *making a promise.*

One night, when I was seventeen years old and in a drunken stupor, I fell down a flight of stairs and crushed two vertebrae and ruptured a disc. I was instantly paralyzed from my waist down. I spent the next six months in the hospital in traction, confined to a Stryker frame. A Stryker frame is one of those beds positioned within a giant wheel with a board under the patient's back and another board on top of the patient's legs, stomach, and chest. The hospital personnel turn the patient over by rotating the wheel.

I can still see the doctor running up and down my leg with that little pinwheel device that looked like a cowboy spur on a stick. As he would run that little wheel down my leg I could see evenly spaced pinpricks of blood on my leg . . . but I couldn't feel a thing. The whole experience was surreal. It was as if the doctor were performing this test on someone else's leg.

One day my parents; our family doctor, Dr. Moberly; and our parish priest, Monsignor Sigwarth—the same priest who "graduated" me from eighth grade, visited me in my hospital room. The mere fact that all of them arrived together told me something significant was about to happen. Dr. Moberly was selected to tell me the bad news. Dr. Moberly proceeded to tell a very frightened seventeen-year-old kid that the x-rays confirmed that I had shattered two vertebrae, collapsed a disc, and damaged my spinal cord. Dr. Moberly went on to tell me that the paralysis was permanent and that I would never walk again. I remember Monsignor Sigwarth telling me that if this were God's will, I needed to accept it.

To this day, I cannot explain the reason for—or the source of—my reaction to this news. I think a normal reaction to news of this nature would be somewhere between the sobbing acceptance of "woe is me" to a sorrowful "why me?" My reaction was neither; instead, it was a violent rejection of the whole idea that I would never walk again. Although the term "denial" was not yet in the medical lexicon of the 1960s, I was about to give it real meaning.

I yelled at the top of my lungs that they were wrong, that I would not be a cripple, and that I would walk again. I refused to listen to their protests that I was being too loud and disturbing other patients. I continued to yell through my tears, "I'll show you!" I created such a scene that they had to sedate me to quiet me down.

When I woke up several hours later, my room was dark, and I was alone. It was in that dark hospital room that I, for the first time in my life, made a promise to myself. In spite of everything Dr. Moberly had told me about my physical condition and the injury I had sustained, I promised myself that I was going to walk out of that hospital under my own power.

The next morning, I threw myself into the physical therapy routine with a newfound source of strength and resolve. Up to that point in my rehabilitation, physical therapy had consisted of some nurse's aide coming into my room for an hour a day, releasing the tension on my traction device, and rubbing my legs, ankles, and feet in an effort to improve their blood circulation.

My new self-created therapy involved attempting to wiggle my toes by using sheer will power. I would take the blanket off my feet and sit up in bed so I could see my toes. While staring at my toes, I would concentrate every drop of energy in my body to get my toes to wiggle. I would concentrate so hard that my face would turn red, veins would bulge on the side of my head, and I would break into a sweat. I would do this exercise as long as I could hold my concentration or my breath, whichever gave in first. I did this over and over and over, all day long.

After the first couple of days, the nurses on the floor noticed what I was doing and encouraged me to stop. When I continued in spite of their advice, they finally informed Dr. Moberly of what I was doing. Dr.

Moberly gave me strict instructions to quit, as he was concerned I was holding out hope when, as he termed it, my situation was hopeless. He said he was afraid that I was creating a false expectation and that I should accept the situation for what it was. He told me that I was wasting my time, that these exercises were draining my energy, and that if I continued, I would prolong my recovery period.

I had previously told Dr. Moberly what I thought of his prognosis, and so this time I decided to tell him what he wanted to hear, while secretly continuing my new therapy. I told him that I would discontinue the exercise, knowing that I was going to continue it when no one was watching. I knew he would instruct the nurse's station to check on me frequently to make sure I was following his advice. To keep from being detected, I changed my tactics. Instead of uncovering my feet, I left them covered with the blanket. I then visualized what they must look like. I also began doing the exercises from a prone position so that I wouldn't be so obvious. When I found this didn't work as well as I wanted, I changed my tactics one more time. The next approach involved doing my exercises during the nighttime hours when the nurses thought the patients were sleeping. I would exercise as much as I could during the night hours and sleep during the day hours.

Two weeks after beginning this exercise program, my toes finally wiggled. The first time I made my toes wiggle, I did not believe that it really had happened. I made them wiggle again and immediately grabbed the nurse's call button that was attached to my bed. I was so excited that I wanted someone else to confirm what I was seeing. The first nurse to come to my room was as excited as I was when I showed her that I could make my toes wiggle. The nurse called Dr. Moberly to share the news, and he said he would check in on me when he made his hospital rounds later in the day.

A couple of hours and a few hundred toe wiggles later, he finally showed up. Like a little kid who had just learned how to tie his own shoes or ride a bike, I wanted to show him what I could do. His reaction was not what I had expected. I thought he would be as excited and happy as I was. Instead, he was cautious and reserved. He said there was no sound medical explanation for the controllable movement he was observing in my toes. He went on to say that even with this controllable movement, I still would never regain the ability to walk. Before I could protest, he pulled the little spur on a stick device out of his jacket pocket and ran it up and down my legs. The silent corroboration of what he had just said was apparent as I watched the painless pin pricks of blood on both of my legs. Though I could move my toes, I still had no feeling in my calves or thighs.

For the second time since I entered the hospital, I cried. In a few short minutes, my emotional pendulum had swung from one extreme of ecstasy to the other extreme of depression. I thought I had accomplished some marvelous feat that was going to take me to full recovery, yet the doctor relegated it to the equivalency of not bothering to attempt to figure out how the magician in a carnival sideshow pulled off his trick. I was seventeen years old and a high school dropout. Dr. Moberly was a fifty-year-old man with twenty-five years of formal education and twenty years of medical practice. Who was I to challenge his opinion?

That night, as I lay in bed feeling sorry for myself and verging on accepting life as paraplegic, I remembered the promise I made to myself two weeks earlier. Every drop of medical science, every opinion of the medical staff, and every test were 100 percent consistent. The damage to my spinal cord was irreversible. Spinal cords cannot and do not heal themselves after a significant trauma. As I tried to think my way through the conflicting proposition, I saw myself imagining a scale, similar to the one Lady Justice holds in her uplifted arm. I could see the whole world and every compelling argument why I should be paralyzed on one side of the scale. I saw my promise to myself sitting alone on the other side of the scale. As I visualized this imaginary scale, I noticed that the side with all the medical evidence was not lower than the other side containing my promise to myself. In fact, the scale was perfectly balanced, with both sides of the scale at the midway point.

At that instant, the epiphany occurred. It was then and there that I realized my promise to myself was just as important as a mountain of medical evidence. At that moment, I learned that outcomes are not always determined by knowledge or education or the capacity to perform logical analysis. Instead, sometimes outcomes are determined by the strength of a person's belief system.

Never Underestimate the Power of the Human Spirit!

That very night, I resumed, with a newfound passion, the exercises that had allowed my toes to wiggle. Only this time, I figured out a new approach. Instead of just concentrating on my toes, I needed to work on my legs. My new approach consisted of scooching my upper body down toward the foot of the bed. I would reach downward with my hands and grab the lowest portion of the bedside rail I could reach. I would then pull with all of my arm strength until I got my body to slide downward. I would repeat the process again and again. The net result was that eventually my feet rested against the railing at the foot of the bed. As I continued to scooch my upper body lower in the bed, it forced my knees to bend upward. Although I couldn't feel my feet resting on the bottom railing, I could see that they were firmly planted. I then concentrated on pushing myself back to my starting position in the bed by straightening out my legs. As I had done with my toes, I would concentrate on the muscles that I thought were involved with straightening my legs. I would concentrate as hard as I could for as long as I could. When I couldn't do it any longer, I would take a break and then resume. Each time one of the nurses would come into my room to bring meals or medicine or to check on me, they would discover me scrunched up at the bottom of the bed. They would ask how I got in such a position, and I would tell them that I must have tossed and turned in my sleep. I don't think I fooled any of the nurses. I think they all were fully aware of what I was doing, and I think they made a deliberate decision to not tell Dr. Moberly this time. Some of the nurses had been in the room when Dr. Moberly dismissed my toe wiggling as inconsequential, and they had seen the look of dejection that had crossed my face. I don't believe any of the nurses actually thought my exercises were going to make a difference in my rehabilitation, but I think they decided to let me try.

By the middle of the third week, I could actually feel my feet pressing against the foot rail at the bottom of the bed. I couldn't get the muscles to begin straightening my legs enough to push my body back up to the top of the bed, but at least I was making real progress. Each day when Dr. Moberly made his rounds, he would stop in and spend a few minutes looking at my chart. He would ask how I was doing, and I would always say, "I'm doing fine, Doc. I am going to walk out of this hospital." He would smile his benign smile as if to say, "Sure you are—about the time pigs fly." I never shared with him any of the progress I was making. I didn't tell him I had regained feeling in the bottom of my feet. He had discontinued doing the test with the spur-on-a-stick device, as I am sure he thought there was no point. If he had continued doing it, he would have noticed me flinching now that I had regained feeling in my feet.

The rest of the recovery happened at a much faster pace than did the initial toe wiggling or foot pressure on the bottom of the bed. Within a few days of regaining feeling in my feet, I started to be able to straighten my knees and push my body back up to the top of the bed using just my legs. I continued to keep my progress a secret because I had made up my mind I wasn't going to tell anyone until I could walk on my own power. I had been totally deflated by Dr. Moberly when he dismissed my toe wiggling, and I was not going to let that happen again.

By the end of the third week, I was ready to attempt getting out of bed and standing up under my own power. That day, I practiced my leg pushes every time I was alone in my room. I was getting good enough at the drill that I could pull myself down toward the bottom of the bed with my hands and then turn right around and push myself up again with my legs. I had also been able to manage to lift my leg and knee up to my chest while lying on my back. The only thing left to do was to scooch my legs off the side of the bed and attempt to stand up while holding on to the bed. I waited until the nurse made her last visit of the night and had turned off the light in my room. I pulled the blanket off my legs and slid them off the side of the bed. I sat on the edge of the bed with my bare feet solidly on the floor for what seemed like an eternity. I didn't want to rush because I knew if it didn't work and I fell, I would never be able to get myself back into bed without the nurses finding out what I had tried to do.

When I was sure I was ready, I slowly started to stand up, all the while holding onto the bed rail with both hands. I was amazed at how much my legs had atrophied in the five months I had been in the hospital. It seemed that both thighs had lost half of their muscle mass, and as I stood there with my legs trembling, I realized that they had also lost much of their strength. After standing at the side of my bed for what was probably only a few seconds, I had to quickly sit back down on the edge of the bed. I rested a few minutes and repeated the process. Each time, I was able to stand at the edge of the bed for a little longer than the previous time. After a couple dozen efforts, I had to lay back in bed and rest. The little bit of exercise had completely worn me out. As exhausted as I had become, I also knew that I had yet to take a step under my own power. I did not want to wait until the next night to try again, so I slid my legs over the side of the bed and this time, stood up only holding on to the rail with one hand. I took a deep breath, and in a stiff-legged motion, I slid my right foot forward. I then shifted my weight from my left leg on to my right leg and slowly slid my left leg forward. I was now far enough away from the bed that I would only be able to take the next step if I released my grip on the bed railing. I let go of the bed rail and stood there—alone and in what seemed like a foreign place. I was no longer connected to the bed to which I had been attached to for over five months. The overhead lights in the hospital room had been turned off earlier by the nurse, and the only light came from the standard hospital night-light. The shadows created by the night-light gave the room an eerie feeling. Contributing to the eeriness was the fact that I was standing on my own two feet—something I had not done for five full months!

The moment of truth was at hand. The next step was going to take me far enough away from the bed that I would not be able to reach the handrail. I slowly moved my foot forward with a stiff-kneed motion, shifted my weight, and in an equally stiff-kneed motion, slid the other foot forward. I had done it! I had walked on my own power. I was now only two events away from keeping the promise I had made to myself. The first thing I had to do was to show Dr. Moberly, because his negative attitude had been my positive motivation. The second thing I had to do was to complete the act of physically walking out of the hospital on my own power.

I knew I wasn't going to get the opportunity to do the second thing for at least a few more days, or even weeks, but there was nothing stopping me from doing the first thing. Even though it was now past midnight, I shuffled back to the side of the bed, and instead of sitting down on the bed, I reached for and pressed the nurse's call button. I knew it would take a minute or two for one of the nurses to come to my room in response to the call button. I then turned around and shuffled away from the bed and toward the door of my room. When I got halfway between the bed and the door, I stopped and waited for the nurse to arrive. I hadn't intended to frighten the nurse, but in hindsight, I can see how frightening it must have been for her. The nurse responded to the call button by entering my room at a fast pace. She was coming from a well-lit hallway and was entering a semi-dark room. Her eyes had not adjusted to the darkness as she crossed the threshold, and a few feet in front of her was standing a person in an open-backed hospital gown. The sudden appearance of a person standing in the middle of a dark room where the only occupant is supposed to be a bed-ridden paraplegic caused her to let out a scream. As her eyes adjusted further to the night-light lit room, she recognized that it was me, and the look on her face changed rapidly from one of fear to befuddlement. While she was regaining her composure and attempting to formulate the right question, chaos was breaking out on this wing of the hospital. Other nurses working at the nurse's station knew she had gone to a patient's room in response to a call button signal and had let out a loud scream shortly thereafter. The nurses, sensing an unspecified emergency, hit the "panic" button at the nurse's station, which immediately notified the floor supervisor and hospital security. The nurses at the nurses' station quickly proceeded to my room to assist their fellow nurse. At the same time, patients who had been sound asleep heard the nurse's scream and were now sticking their heads out the doors of their respective hospital rooms to see what had happened. The other patients' sense of excitement was heightened by the sound of nurses and security staff all running to a patient's room.

For the last five months of being bedridden, "open-backed" hospital gowns seemed like a pretty good idea. Now that I was standing in the middle of a room that was rapidly filling up with nurses and security staff, it seemed like less of a good idea. With one hand behind my back attempting to hold the flaps of my gown together, and while standing on rapidly exhausting and trembling legs, I now found myself facing a group of professionals who were trained to react to almost any conceivable situation yet now stood frozen in their tracks. The nurses in the room were all familiar with my case. I had been on that particular floor long enough that all of them had, on occasion, tended to my needs at one time or another. I could see the confusion and conflict in their eyes. The first reaction of a nurse is to get the patient back into the safety and security of his bed—yet in my case, they couldn't figure out how it was that I happened to be out of bed, standing in the middle of the room, and the further conflict of, "If he suffers from paralysis, isn't it a good thing that he is standing in the middle of the room?"

Two weeks later, I walked out of the hospital on my own power.

"Promises Are More Powerful Than Goals"

RULE # 3:

Clearly Identify Your Promise.

Imagination is more important than knowledge.

—Albert Einstein

The future has several names.
For the weak—it is the impossible.
For the fainthearted—it is the unknown.
For the thoughtful and valiant—it is the ideal.
—Victor Hugo

Progress has little to do with speed, but much to do with direction.

—Anonymous

All our dreams come true if we have the courage to pursue them.

—Walt Disney

To hit a target, first you must see it clearly.

—Bill Bartmann

A goal is a dream with a deadline.

—Ken Blanchard

All things will work together for your good.

—Romans 8:28

Once you decide what YOU want to do or become or achieve, you must define your promise, your objective—the thing you want to accomplish—with a high degree of clarity and specificity. The more specifically defined the target is, the easier it will be to achieve. You cannot hit a target unless you can clearly identify it. The childhood game of pin the tail on the donkey demonstrates how difficult it is to try to hit a target you can't see. Once the blindfold has been removed and the target is clearly visible, pinning the tail in the right location is remarkably simple. Trying to accomplish an objective that is poorly defined is like an archer trying to hit the bull's-eye of a target he can't see.

Imagine yourself standing at the twenty-yard line of a football stadium with a bow and a quiver full of arrows in your hand. Twenty yards away in the end zone is an archery target. As you shoot your first arrow, you will note whether you are shooting too high, too low, too much to the right, or too much to the left. Your second arrow will then be adjusted accordingly to correct the previous error. Your third arrow will be adjusted even more precisely. After each shot, you will take what you have learned from the previous shots and make your future adjustments accordingly. With this constant adjustment for error, you will eventually be able to hit the target.

Now imagine yourself standing in the same place, only this time, before you get to shoot your first arrow, someone puts a blindfold over your eyes and spins you around several times. Although you know the target is out there somewhere, you don't have a clue as to which direction you should shoot your arrow. You will be forced to shoot your arrows in the general direction where you thought the target was located before you were spun around. Not only are you unable to see the target, you can't see where your arrows are going, so you can't make any worthwhile adjustments. Your chances of hitting the target have been greatly reduced by one simple factor: *you can't see the target.* All you can hope to do is to get lucky. All of the other factors remained exactly the same: you still have the same bow, the same number of arrows, and the same distance to the target. This one factor, namely *being able to clearly identify the target,* has made all the difference in the world.

If you want to achieve an objective, you also must have a clearly identified target.

The narrower and the more specific you can make your promise, the better.

Examples:

- An average golfer will aim for the green. A professional golfer will aim for the flag.

- Mel Gibson, in the movie *The Patriot,* tells his son, "Aim small— miss small."

- The corollary to Mel's advice is: if you aim big, you may miss big.

When I have asked some people to identify their promise, they respond with answers like, "I want to be rich," "I want to be famous," or "I want to make a lot of money and have a lot of fun."

When I hear descriptions like this, I then ask: "How rich?" "How famous?" "How much money is 'a lot'?" "What is 'fun'?"

Almost always, my question is met with a blank look on the person's face. Very few people have a reply. Some people attempt a reply with whatever comes to mind—and it is obvious to both of us that up to that moment in time, they had never really tried to clearly identify what they think they want.

Like the pin the tail on the donkey game or the archery example I used, unless you can specifically answer this question, you really don't even have a target to shoot at.

RULE # 4:

Identify Your Personal Motivator.

Turn your wounds into wisdom.

—Oprah Winfrey

Success is the greatest revenge of all. There is nothing you can say or do that will irritate your detractors more.

—Bill Bartmann

A successful person is one who can lay a firm foundation with the bricks that others have thrown at him or her.

—David Brinkley

Never avenge yourself, but leave the way open for God's wrath.

—Romans 12:19

Don't forgive your enemies for their sake—do it for your sake.

—Bill Bartmann

Think of a person whose name can invoke either a positive or negative image in your mind. You can strive for an objective in order to please someone or, in the alternative, to show someone. When you think of your promise, who is the person you are doing it for? Who is the person you want to show you can do this? Although a book on positive thinking will rarely extol the virtues of a negative, there are occasions when a negative personal motivator will help you accomplish a positive objective. There are times when a negative personal motivator is stronger (and more effective) than a positive personal motivator.

Identifying a personal motivator will provide an emotional reaction and additional energy to help you accomplish your promise. Both of these will be especially helpful during any frustration cycles you might encounter.

If you can identify more than one personal motivator, that is all the better. The more reasons you have for wanting to accomplish this promise, the easier it will be for you to stay focused on the target.

Several years ago, *Forbes* magazine interviewed me on the very question of my personal motivator. I responded that I had different personal motivators for each of my separate promises. Some of the motivators were positive in nature, and some of them were negative in nature. I shared with *Forbes* an example of each.

I used a negative motivator to help me get through college. Kathy's older sister Connie has, over the forty years I have known her, become a dear friend and a steadfast supporter. I truly love this woman for who and what she is. Our relationship, however, wasn't always this way. Early in the dating relationship between Kathy and me, Connie gave her younger sister some sisterly advice when she accurately told Kathy that as a high school dropout, a gang member, and a fellow more interested in drinking beer and getting into fights, I probably wouldn't amount to much. When I started college, those words still haunted me. Perhaps because I was afraid she might be right. I then and there determined, "I am going to prove her wrong." Kathy's sister Connie became my personal motivator and is probably responsible for my making it through college. This motivator could only be classified as negative because I wasn't doing this "for someone," I was doing this to "show someone."

While I was in college, my study desk faced the wall in my bedroom. I wrote Connie's name on a 3x5 index card and taped it on the wall directly in front of me at eye level. This way, each time I looked up, I saw her name and that reminded me that I needed to prove her wrong. Each night as I would become tired and get ready to quit studying for the evening, I would naturally raise my head. Each time, I would see Connie's name on the card in front of me . . . and I would lower my head and study some more. As I said, Connie is probably the main reason I finished college. Without that additional motivation, I would have studied a lot less, and since I managed to graduate by the skin of my teeth, it turns out that I needed every bit of motivation I had mustered. Connie first learned of that index card twenty-five years later when *Forbes* published that story.

RULE # 5:

Create a Promise Plan.

By failing to prepare—you are preparing to fail.

—Benjamin Franklin

The beginning is the most important part of the work.

—Plato

The world makes way for the man who knows where he is going.

—Ralph Waldo Emerson

Be constantly renewed in the spirit of your mind, having a fresh mental and spiritual attitude.

—Ephesians 4:22

The man who is prepared for his battle has his battle half fought.

—Miguel de Cervantes

Focus on your strengths—not your weaknesses.

—Bill Bartmann

When we discussed Rule #3, specifically identifying your promise, I said Rule #5 would make that task easier.

Every successful business has a written business plan. I realize this is a universal statement because I used the word "every" in the sentence. I am very aware that it is exceedingly rare that any universal statement is always accurate. I am, however, willing to wager that this is one of those rare times when a universal statement is true. In my forty years of doing business in the United States and abroad, in all of my dealings from Wall Street to Silicon Valley to Main Street America, and from my experiences with small businesses to billion-dollar-a-year businesses, I have never come across a successful business that didn't have a well-thought-out business plan.

The mere creating, writing, and reviewing of a business plan helps the businessperson understand clearly where he or she is going, how to get there, when it will happen, who will be needed along the way, what it will take, and what the reward will be when the objective is met. Now, aren't those the very same questions you will need to know about your promise—if you hope to achieve it?

In this section, we are going to create the equivalent of a business plan, only it will be not for any existing business; instead, it will be for you and your promise. The one we will create for you will not be as extensive as that of a Fortune 500 company's; in fact, we will probably be able to get yours all down on one sheet of paper.

We won't call this a business plan because it really isn't. Instead, we will call it what it really is—a promise plan. It will be one page with everything you need to know about how to achieve your promise. Depending on the size and the scope of your promise—some of you may actually need a second page at some point in time.

Now, before we get to the actual creation of your promise plan, let tell you why this is important (if the previous business plan reason didn't already persuade you).

There are two reasons for writing down your plan.

The first reason is that an objective created in your mind is a "thought." Our brain processes "thoughts" the same way it does information provided by our senses; the more we can reinforce (identify) this objective in our brain, the clearer the target will be. The mere act of writing it out will cause you to focus on this promise. It also allows your other senses to become involved as we use touch to write and sight to see and record this target you have set for yourself. The human mind receives its information from our various senses. The more senses we can involve in identifying our objective, the more assistance the mind can and will provide.

The second reason you must write it down is that the mere exercise of writing it down will require you to clarify not only the objective but also other things that will be crucial if you are to succeed in your quest.

While it is important to write it down, simply writing it down as a statement isn't enough. We need to show our mind how it is that we are going to accomplish this objective. Remember, the mind will not allow us to do something it thinks we cannot do (it wants to save us from the embarrassment and humiliation of failure), and conversely, our mind will allow (and help) us do those things that it thinks we are capable of accomplishing.

So if we want to prevent our mind from frustrating our attempt—and at the same time want to create an environment in which our mind will help us accomplish our objective—we need to persuade our mind that we can do whatever it is we have set down as our objective.

By going through the drill I am about to describe, we accomplish two things: first, we narrowly define the target, so the mind gets a very clear picture of just what it is we are trying to accomplish, rather than some big, ambiguous picture of a large objective that would be difficult to attain. Second, by going through the steps you are about to see, the mind can rationally conclude that the target we have set for ourselves is indeed attainable so long as we follow the indicated steps. Once the mind is persuaded that the objective can be achieved, it has no reason to serve as an "overprotective" mother and attempt to shield us from potential embarrassment. Instead, when it sees the benefits that will flow from attaining the stated objective, it will be further persuaded that it should help us accomplish this objective—as it clearly is in our best self-interest—which, remember, is the primary function of the mind itself.

Here are the seven focus points you must write down if you want to persuade your mind to help you accomplish your objective.

WHAT:

- This is the single statement that narrowly describes your objective.

- It should be no more than one or two sentences long.

- It should be as narrow and as specific as you can possibly make it.

- Take a moment and think about your objective. Write a sentence or two that best describes what it is you wish to accomplish.

- When I do this part of the exercise in my lectures or workshops, I tell people to use a pencil because by the time they are done answering the six questions that follow, they most likely will be making some changes to this objective.

- Don't let the fact that you may be able to better define your objective at a later point in time keep you from writing it down. For the time being, write down your objective as you know it. Give credit to your "gut" reaction.

WHEN:

- This is the date by which you plan to successfully accomplish the objective set forth in WHAT above.

- An objective without a delivery timeline is merely idle or wishful thinking.

- Set a deadline for the accomplishment of the objective as well as a deadline for each of the steps you have identified as necessary to accomplish this objective. As you set these deadlines, be realistic and fair to yourself. Be sure you have the time to commit, or be prepared to make the time.

- If your objective is to be accomplished in phases, stages, or sequential intervals (one step after another), then identify the date to accomplish each of the sequential steps. Place a special focus on the date you intend to accomplish the first of these several steps.

- It is important to establish a time line for accomplishing our first objective so we can have an accurate measuring device to see if we are on schedule. If you are off target accomplishing the first step, by definition you will become off target to accomplish the following steps.

- It isn't fatal to have an accomplishment take longer than you originally thought. Once you see the new time line, you can then adjust all of the other components of your promise plan to compensate for the new schedule.

WHERE:

- Where will this happen? Where will you be? Write down the specific physical location where you think the event will occur and where you will be when it does.

- By adding location, you automatically add all of the trappings— the sights, the sounds, the smells, the experiences, the history, and the emotions that have been previously recorded by your mind, regarding that particular location.

- No matter where you pick, you (and your mind) already have a full database of sensory experiences associated with that location. When you think of your workplace, you think of more than just the building that houses it. You immediately think of sights and sounds you associate with that particular location.

- The same is true for the other locations that are special to you, whether your kitchen, the beach, a summer home, a vacation spot, a girlfriend's house, or your parents' home.

- By identifying a specific location, you add clarity, reality, and substance to the target you are now shooting for. Your mind begins to see and feel where, when, and what you are going to accomplish. The more the mind can see and believe, the more real it becomes in your mind's database. This will help you envision the result, and it serves as a pleasant motivator.

WHY:

- Write down why you want this objective. It isn't enough to want it or to wish that it would happen. To accomplish this objective, you will need to be motivated. As we discussed in Rule #4, people generally want to accomplish an objective for one of two reasons. They either do it *for someone,* or they do it to *show someone.*

- Answer the question honestly: why do you want to achieve this objective?

- Remember as you answer this question and the others that follow that this is your promise plan—not anyone else's. It therefore is crucial that your answers reflect the answers that suit you best, and not what you think someone else would have you write down.

WHO:

- Who will benefit from your achieving your objective?

- First, whose situation or life will have improved once you accomplish this objective? Will it be yours, your family's, your boss's, your company's, or society's?

- The second WHO is who you will need to help you accomplish your promise. Everyone needs help from someone. If your promise is one that will require the assistance of others, or skills and knowledge that you do not currently posses, identify who and what it will take to achieve this promise, and list how you will gain these missing elements. Begin to think about whom you will need on your side if you are to succeed.

- Again, it doesn't matter what someone else might write down—the only answer that will work for you is your own.

HOW:

- How do you think you will you do this? What are the steps that will be necessary to take you from where you are to where you want to go?

- Most people have difficulty with this question because of all the questions. This is the one that most people have thought about the least. It is okay if you don't already know the whole plan or all the steps that are going to be necessary. Write down the steps you do know and think will be necessary. Even if they are incomplete at the present time, you will have started to build the framework. As you move forward and begin to gain new information, you will be able to revise this section.

- The secret of achieving big is thinking small! Significant objectives are rarely, if ever, accomplished in a single step. Significant objectives require a logical, step-by-step plan that will take you from where you are now to where you want to be.

- Write a plan of action identifying the steps you will have to take to reach your promise. Use as much detail as you can. Each step needs to be in logical order. Let your small successes carry you to your ultimate objective. Use as much detail as you can (the more the better). If at first you can't think of all the steps, just make an outline listing the ones that come to mind. You can update the list as you review it.

- If I am unsure of all of the steps that I will need to take in order to accomplish a particular objective, I start at the end and move backward. Instead of starting at the beginning and trying to figure out all of the individual steps between here and the end, I do it the other way around. By starting at the end, I can clearly see what it is I want to achieve. I then ask myself, "What was the last step I had to accomplish to end up with this objective?" When I ask myself that question, the answer becomes fairly easy to figure out. I then repeat the process, moving backward with each step, until I get to where I am now.

- It really isn't as complicated as it sounds. In fact, most people to whom I have taught this technique tell me it is easier. They say it is easier than they expected because if you try to go from here to there, you will encounter a wide variety of choices and decisions, any one of which could be compared to a fork-in-the-road where you could end up going down the wrong path for a long time before you finally realize it. By starting at the end and moving toward the beginning, you have fewer choices. It is much like trying to figure out a maze. If you start from the beginning, mazes can be very challenging. If you start from the center (the end) and attempt to find your way to the beginning, it is much simpler.

HOW IT WILL MAKE YOU FEEL:

- The answer to this question really doesn't provide much substance to the plan or how you are going to accomplish it, but it does add some very powerful motivation. Having thought about how accomplishing this objective will make you feel will add another source of data for your subconscious mind to process when it thinks about this.

- This is explained in more detail in Rule #9 where I talk about mental-vision.

The first thing that happens to people when they go through these steps is that they discover that the thing they had previously thought they wanted isn't necessarily the thing they now have specifically identified! As you force yourself to think not just about the objective you have in mind, but also about all of the things that are required to accomplish it, you gain a much clearer focus of just what you want.

Here is an example of a person I recently took through this process. When we began, I asked him his objective, and he said:

"I want to make a lot of money and have a lot of fun."

After I asked him to define "a lot of money" and "lot of fun," he admitted he didn't have a certain amount of money in mind and really couldn't define what "a lot of fun" meant. As we talked, he said, "I want to make a lot of money, so I can enjoy the rest of my life" (he is in his mid-fifties). I told him that some people might think he had conflicting goals, as making a lot of money usually takes time and hard work, and yet half of his goal was to enjoy the rest of his life, which I assumed meant he would want to be comfortably retired. I explained that if he were willing to commit all of the time necessary to make "a lot of money," he might have to postpone his retirement, or worse, all the hard work necessary to get "a lot of money" could wear him out before he retired. After he thought about it a bit, he said, "I'm fifty-five, and I plan on living until I am eighty, which means I have twenty-five years left. I want to make enough money in the next five years that I can retire when I am sixty and live comfortably for the last twenty."

By going through this process, he was able to figure out how much money he would need (plus a little bit in case he made it past eighty) to live on during the last twenty years. He also figured out how he could generate that same sum of money over the next five years (now that he knew how long he had to raise the money) so he could have "lots of fun" the last twenty years of his life.

Before we started on the process, he knew what he wanted, but he just didn't have it in focus. Because it was out of focus, his odds of achieving it were pretty remote. Once he went through the process and completed his promise plan, he could see clearly that what he wanted, needed more definition.

This man is not unusual. If anything, he is really like 90 percent of the people I visit with about their objectives. They have a general idea of what they want, but they never sat down and thought about each detail. Once they do, the objective becomes much more clear and much more obtainable.

RULE # 6:
Review the Promise Plan Regularly.

*The future belongs to those who believe in the beauty
of their dreams.*

—Eleanor Roosevelt

Opportunity meets you at your level of expectation.

—Bill Bartmann

By all means, don't say, "if I can," say "I will."

—Abraham Lincoln

*And all things, whatsoever ye shall ask in prayer, believing,
ye shall receive.*

—Matthew 21:22

*Obstacles are those frightful things you see when you take
your eye off your goals.*

—Anonymous

One of the simplest, and yet most important, secrets of achieving an objective is to keep it in sight. We have all heard expressions "keep your eye on the prize" or "stay focused." Of all of the secrets of success, this one is the most overlooked, most under appreciated, and most misunderstood.

The human mind is a marvelous and powerful device. In the last one hundred and fifty years, we have begun to unravel some of its mystery, yet we still know so little about the mechanics of how it works and how it does what it does. In the last twenty years or so, we have discovered that the human brain has over a *million million* nerve cells (no, that's not a typo or a mistakenly repeated word—the human brain really does have one million million nerve cells). The total number of synapses in the cortex of one person is 10 to the 15th power (10,000,000,000,000,000), or about 200,000 times the total population of us humans on earth. Numbers such as these are simply incomprehensible for most of us. Although we don't fully understand how it does what it does, we do know that the human mind is more complicated than any supercomputer ever devised and is faster and more efficient than any as well.

By staying focused through reinforcing our desire to achieve, accomplish or obtain this prize that has become the object of our promise, we enlist our mind to help us accomplish our objective. Remember earlier when we discussed that the primary function of the subconscious mind is self-preservation? We discussed how this desire to protect us sometimes put the subconscious mind in the role of an overprotective mother attempting to keep us from engaging in any activity that might cause us harm, pain, or embarrassment. Here, the opposite happens. In the context of helping us achieve an objective that is good for us—hence one that is consistent with self-preservation—it is consistent with the subconscious mind's mission to help us. We now have this supercomputer mind helping us, not hindering us.

We have learned from our prior life experiences that if we concentrate on something—stay focused on something and continue to think about something—eventually we begin to find a solution. This solution didn't come to our attention by voodoo or magic, but rather, as we focused on a particular desired result, we sent continuous and repeated messages to our mind that we were looking for a particular solution. Eventually, our mind showed us the solution we were seeking.

There are three distinct but equally important ways we can stay focused on our objective—the promise plan, the *visual reminder*, and the pocket promise™. The more of these we utilize, the more signals we send to our subconscious to assist us in finding the solution. Let's take a look at them.

PROMISE PLAN

You have already prepared your promise plan. Now put your promise plan where you will see it on a regular basis. Some people put their promise plan with their checkbook or their stack of household bills waiting to be paid. By doing so, they know that they will both see and touch their promise plan at least once a month, if not more often. Since the promise plan is the detailed business plan of what, how, when, where, and why, as we review it from time to time, we have the opportunity to revise anything that needs revision.

I have my promise plan in the front pocket of a notebook I carry with me every day. I don't look at it every day, but I do pull it out at least once every week or two to see if I am on track and on schedule. I make at least some minor revision every time I review it. There are occasions when something new has happened or new information has come to my attention that causes me to make a major or minor revision.

VISUAL REMINDER

A visual reminder is anything that will remind you or motivate you to work to accomplish your promise.

Put your visual reminder in a place where you will have to see it daily. Find the location suited to you where you will see it most often. Put reminders of your promise in many locations throughout your home or office.

Visual reminders are limited only by our imagination. Here are examples some people have successfully used.

Index cards:

- This index card can contain the name of your personal motivator (positive or negative), or it can have anything else you choose to write on it—so long as your reaction to it will be motivational.

- You can put this index card in a wide range of locations—you decide what's best:

  - The bathroom mirror, so you see it every morning as you get ready for work.

  - The bedroom wall, as I did with the note card with my sister-in-law's name, so that I would see it every time I got up from my study desk.

  - The wall of your office or work cubicle, so you are reminded of it frequently during the course of your workday.

- In a picture frame on your desk; just because it is a picture frame, don't think that you can't put an index card in it.

- Taped to your desk, next to the phone, so you will see it every time you pick up the phone. ·

- The dashboard of your car.

Posters:

If you can find a pictorial representation of your objective, put this picture in the place where you spend most of your time. If you can have the picture enlarged, even to the point of becoming a mural on your wall, do it!

A person who has become a good personal friend first came to work for me in 1991. During the initial job interview, I asked him what his goal in life was. He said he had always wanted to go on a camera safari in Africa. He said it was his goal to take such a trip someday. A few months later, after he had started his employment with me, I asked him again what his goal in life was. He again replied that it was to go on a camera safari in Africa. I then asked him if he was any closer to that goal today than he was a few months earlier when I had asked him the first time. He said he wasn't. I then asked him what he had done in the last several months to make that goal a reality. He admitted that he hadn't really had time to think about it too much and that he hadn't done anything in the intervening months to move toward his goal. I then asked him if he was really serious about the trip, to which he replied he was. I then told him that if he was to accomplish this goal, he was going to have to think about it every day, and that if he did that, even if only for a few minutes each day, he would eventually learn the way to make it happen. I then suggested that he go to the local travel agency and pick up all the literature he could obtain from them on the various trip options. I also told him that it was crucial that while he was visiting the travel agency, he should obtain from them one of their posters of Africa. Every travel agency has posters adorning their walls advertising the exotic vacation packages they offer. These posters are really advertising for the location they represent. I knew that if he obtained one of these posters, the picture displayed on it would be consistent with the widely held view of what people think when they think of Africa.

I then told him that I wanted him to hang this poster on the wall opposite his desk so that he would see it every time he looked up from his desk. Although I didn't tell him about the note card (with Kathy's sister's name on it) that got me through college, this really was the same technique, only with a positive motivator instead of a negative motivator.

Less than a year later, he and his wife made their first camera safari to Africa. I say first because since then, they have made two more trips to Africa.

Photographs:

Photographs can be excellent visual reminders. For most of my adult life, I've been fascinated by private airplanes—both as a means of conducting business in a faster, more efficient manner (rather than flying commercial), and as a measure or benchmark of success. I figure that if a company owns their own aircraft, this says two things, both of which equal success in my book. It means that they have plenty of business that requires them to travel extensively and frequently. It also means that they are making enough profit to afford a very expensive vehicle.

Ten years ago, my company owned a small eight-passenger airplane. It was just fine for the type of business we were then conducting, and it was plenty comfortable as well as efficient. Our plane was a Cessna 421, which was a propeller-driven aircraft that we had purchased used for $125,000. It was a single-pilot aircraft and only cost about $500 an hour to operate. As we would fly in and out of airports around the country, I would notice private jets sitting on the runways. Private jets cost anywhere from a couple of million dollars up to $25 to $35 million, and are two-pilot aircraft that can cost as much as $10,000 an hour to operate. The difference isn't a little difference it is a HUGE difference. Almost any reasonably successful company can afford a small airplane—only the best and most profitable companies can afford a private jet. Once I had concluded that only the best and most profitable companies can afford a private jet, I made my promise to get one.

I reasoned that if I could make our company so successful that it needed to do the type of travel requiring a jet aircraft, and I could make our company so successful that it could financially afford such an aircraft, it would be a tremendous accomplishment. The reward for doing so would be the ownership of a private jet—my personal benchmark of success.

I immediately called in members of my senior management team and announced that we were going to buy a jet. The first person to speak up was our chief financial officer, who was quick to remind me that our company was doing well enough to afford the plane we had, but it didn't need—nor could it even remotely afford—the expense of a jet aircraft. I responded that I agreed with him, and that we did not need, and could not afford one . . . yet. I went on to tell him and the others assembled that it was my intention to make the company successful enough and profitable enough that it would soon both need and be able to afford such a luxury. When he looked at me and said, "How are you going to do that?" I replied, "I don't have the foggiest idea—yet—but I know that if doing so will allow me to get a jet aircraft, I'll figure it out."

I then contacted Cessna Aviation in Kansas, the company that makes the Citation II jet aircraft. I told them I was interested in purchasing a jet in the near future and that I wanted them to send me any marketing brochures they had containing pictures of the various models. In the next day's mail, I had two dozen pictures of various makes and models. I sent someone to the local department store to buy me a 10x12 picture frame. I then took one of the pictures that I liked the best, inserted it in the picture frame, and put it on the corner of my desk . . . right next to the picture of my wife and daughters.

That picture stayed on the corner of my desk for the next eighteen months. During this time, whenever I looked up from whatever I was working on, I would see a picture of my wife and daughters and a shiny jet aircraft. I am not ashamed to say that I don't know which picture motivated me the most; honestly, there were probably days that it would be one or the other. In my mind, they were interconnected. I reasoned that if we could afford such a toy, then my wife and daughters would enjoy the up-tick in lifestyle as well.

Eighteen months after first making the announcement to my senior management and putting the picture on my desk, our company had grown to such an extent that it now both needed and could afford a jet aircraft. We purchased a used Citation II jet for slightly more than $1,000,000. I took the picture out of the frame and put the frame in my desk drawer.

Two months later, we were on a flight in the Citation II from New York, back home to Tulsa, Oklahoma. The pilot came back to the rear of the aircraft to tell me that because of stiff headwinds, we were going to need to stop for fuel on the way home. I asked him if there were any alternatives, and he responded, "Just one—you can buy a bigger jet that has more fuel reserves." When we landed in Tulsa, I told him to get me a picture of the type of jet he thought would do the job. The next day, he showed up with a picture of a Gulfstream II. Our Citation II had cost $1 million; the price tag on the Gulfstream II was $5 million, and way over our budget.

The next morning, I huddled our management team. I told them the story, showed them the picture, and told them that we all needed to get back to work so we could afford the Gulfstream II. I pulled the empty picture frame out of my desk drawer, put the picture of the Gulfstream II in the frame, and put the frame back on the corner of my desk. One year later, the company had again grown sufficiently to both need and afford a bigger jet.

When we purchased the Gulfstream II, I really thought we had purchased our last jet. It was fast, it was spacious, and it had fuel range to reach each coast. What I didn't know then was that our business would go international, and we would open an office in England. The Gulfstream II wasn't suited for trans-Atlantic crossings. I pulled the picture frame out of my desk drawer where it had been stored since the date of the purchase of the Gulfstream II. I inserted a picture of a Gulfstream IV—a $20 million aircraft well suited for Atlantic crossings. One year later, we sold our Gulfstream II to Senator Diane Feinstein of California and purchased a Gulfstream IV—with cash.

POCKET PROMISE

A pocket promise is a small (business card-sized) laminated card with your promise printed on one side and our trademarked logo and the words POCKET PROMISE on the other. Each pocket promise we prepare and send will be autographed by me personally because I want you to know that I am aware of the promise you made. You will appreciate the relevancy of that when you get to Rule #8. You can order your pocket promise online by accessing our Web site at www.billbartmann.com.

When you order the pocket promise from us, we will send you a dozen of them. Again, when we get to Rule #8, you will see why you will need more than one.

Since women frequently wear clothing without pockets, the female version of the pocket promise is smaller and can be attached to a key chain. It accomplishes the same purpose; each time you pick up the car keys, you are reminded of your promise.

If you would prefer to make your own pocket reminder, any local Quick-Print or printing franchise will print whatever message you give them on a blank business card. Once you have your objective printed on the card, print a dozen of them and have each of them laminated.

Carrying this pocket promise in your pocket each day will serve as a constant reminder of your promise. Do not put it in your billfold, money clip, or purse. Put it in your pocket, so you will feel it and be reminded of it every time you stick you hand in your pocket. You will be reminded again every evening when you empty out your pockets before hanging up your clothes for the evening. You will be reminded every morning when you gather up the billfold, comb, handkerchief, or whatever else you habitually stick in one or more of your pockets. Coming in contact with your promise several times during the day will keep it fresh in your mind and will cause you to focus on it.

RULE # 7:

TELL YOURSELF THAT YOU WILL SUCCEED

The size of your success is determined by the size of your beliefs.

—David Schwartz

Quit talking about what you can't do—and start talking about what you CAN do.

—Bill Bartmann

According to your faith, be it done to you.

—Matthew 9:29

Believe and act as if it were impossible to fail.

—Charles F. Kettering

Whether you think you can or think you can't—you are right!

—Henry Ford

It is not only important that you believe you can accomplish your objective, it is also important to tell yourself that you will accomplish your objective. This positive affirmation becomes a source of data that your mind can now call upon if and when it develops doubts about accomplishing this objective.

Remember, we are trying to get more positive information into our mind's database to replace and outweigh any negatives that have been previously placed there. We should attempt to send positive messages as often as we can.

This conversation with yourself can be either verbal or nonverbal. You can engage in nonverbal conversations with yourself at almost any time or place. At worst, people will think you are distracted or have a blank look on your face.

When you engage in verbal conversations with yourself, you engage one more of the senses—the sense of hearing. The mere fact that you rarely (if ever) engage in verbal conversations with yourself sends an additional signal to the subconscious and to the file clerk. The message is, "This is unusual. Therefore, I had better take note of it." The net effect is to artificially create an emotional attachment to go with the words you are about to utter. As we learned earlier, the more emotional significance we can attach to a statement, the stronger it will be when recalled by the mind. This becomes a great time to attempt adding as much emotion to your conversation as you can muster. Remember, the file clerk isn't going to be checking the sincerity or the insincerity of the emotional attachment but merely filing it based on the presence of the emotional attachment.

California's governor, Arnold Schwarzenegger, was recently quoted in the *Washington Post* as saying that back in his bodybuilding days when he would be on stage with ten other muscular guys, he was never worried or rattled because he knew the judges would pick the one who says, "I deserve to be the winner because I am the best . . . it's a very calming feeling . . . knowing that you're on the right track and that all [it is], is just a matter of time and effort."

What Arnold is saying is that you should expect to win and that you should expect to succeed. You should tell yourself that you are going to win. You shouldn't be surprised when you win; if anything, you should be shocked if you lose. You should so strongly expect to win that failure is truly not an option.

By telling yourself that you are sure that you will achieve your objective, you gain a newfound sense of confidence that will help you accomplish the very objective you seek.

As you move toward your objective, there will be plenty of times when self-confidence can and might make all the difference in the world. In the mid-90s, our company had a $20 million line of credit with a financial institution. We saw an opportunity to greatly expand our business. To take advantage of the new opportunity, we would need to increase our credit line from $20 million to $80 million. The financial institution we were presently using didn't have the capacity to increase the size of our loan from $20 million to $80 million. Our only alternative was to seek out a new financial institution that would be able to handle the larger loan request.

A loan broker managed to arrange a meeting for us with the J.P. Morgan Bank in New York City. Since this was one of the largest banks in the world, we were confident that they had the capacity to lend us a much larger sum of money. When the broker told us about the potential meeting, he informed us that J.P. Morgan had a reputation for demanding a piece of the ownership of any company to whom they lent substantial money. I told the broker that I would never consent to giving up any ownership of my company and, instead, told the broker that he was authorized to offer J.P. Morgan a higher-than-normal interest rate.

Several weeks later, the broker informed us that J.P. Morgan would be interested in discussing an $80 million loan and that they would waive an equity ownership provision in exchange for a much higher interest rate on the borrowed money. We told the broker to set up the meeting.

The meeting was scheduled for a Monday morning at the J.P. Morgan New York headquarters. When my chief financial officer and I arrived, we were ushered into a very large boardroom where we were met by no fewer than twelve vice presidents and managing directors of the bank. There we were—the two of us and twelve of them. Normally, I don't intimidate very easily, but this got dangerously close. Each one of them was dressed in the conservative dark suit/dark necktie uniform of J.P. Morgan. Most of them wore wire-rimmed glasses, and they all looked and talked like they just stepped out the best and brightest graduate schools in America—because they did. Two hayseeds from Tulsa, Oklahoma, on one side of the table, and twelve Harvard and Wharton MBAs on the other side of the table.

I spent the next hour pitching our deal. I told these bankers about our company, what we did, how we did it, what we were going to do with the money we wanted to borrow and how we would pay them back. When I finished with my presentation, they politely asked if my chief financial officer and I would mind stepping into an adjoining waiting room while they discussed our loan request.

About twenty minutes later, they sent someone to invite us back to the boardroom. After we resumed our seats at the board table, the senior representative of J.P. Morgan informed us that after much consideration, they had agreed to our request for an $80 million loan, but there was one condition—the bank wanted 20 percent ownership in my company. While trying to keep my composure, I told them about the discussion I had with the loan broker and his assurance that J.P. Morgan would waive that requirement in exchange for a higher interest rate and that J.P. Morgan had agreed to this exchange before I agreed to come to this meeting. The banker smiled and said, "Yes, we did previously agree, but we have changed our mind and feel that a 20 percent ownership interest would be appropriate for an $80 million loan." Mustering all the confidence I could dredge up, I reached across the table, shook his hand, and said, "If you change your mind, let me know." I then calmly picked up my papers from their board table, put them in my briefcase, walked around the table, shook hands with each person, and thanked them for their time.

As my CFO and I were leaving the boardroom, I whispered, "Don't look nervous, and whatever you do, don't look back." The two of us walked down the hall heading for the elevator. When I was sure that no one had followed us out of the room, I said "If we are really lucky, someone from that meeting will be sent to catch us before we exit the building." As we punched the elevator button and waited for the elevator to show up, we anxiously listened for the sound of footsteps coming from the direction of the boardroom. Finally, the elevator door opened, and without looking back, we stepped in and waited for the door to close. Once we were alone in the elevator, heading down to the first floor, I looked at my CFO and said, "Our last chance is for them to catch us before we hit the front door, so when we get out of the elevator, walk *slowly* toward the door."

Although we walked as slowly as we could without drawing attention to ourselves, we eventually came to the security checkpoint at the front door of the building. As we were clearing security, we heard a voice calling our names. As we looked back, it was one of the junior members who had been in our meeting. As he approached us—slightly winded since he had taken the steps down from the ninth floor—he said, "They would like you to come back; they think they can work this out." Without cracking a smile, we looked at him and said, "Okay."

As we reentered the boardroom, the senior banker said, "You really would have walked away—wouldn't you?" I said, "Yes, sir. I know the future potential of my company, and I could never give away 20 percent for an $80 million loan." He smiled and said, "Your confidence just got you a loan." We sat back down and finished the negotiations. They made us the $80 million loan at a reduced interest rate without taking any equity ownership in our company!

RULE # 8:

TELL OTHERS OF YOUR PROMISE.

No one succeeds alone.

—Bill Bartmann

If you want something you've never had, you have to do something you've never done.

—Mike Murdock

Keep away from people who try to belittle your ambitions. Small people always do that, but the really great make you feel that you, too, can become great.

—Mark Twain

Death and life are in the power of the tongue [words], and you will eat the fruit thereof.

—Proverbs 18:21

People may doubt what you say, but they will believe what you do.

—Anonymous

It has been my observation that most people get ahead during the time other people waste.

—Henry Ford

When William the Conqueror landed on the coast of England prior to the battle of Hastings in 1066, he commanded his troops to burn the boats that had carried them across the English Channel. He knew that he could win the battle only if his troops were totally committed. He also knew that if they recognized that there could be no retreat, they would find a way to succeed. William the Conqueror won that battle.

The lesson to be learned from William the Conqueror is that once you are fully committed to a plan of action, your subconscious mind will help you find a way to accomplish the plan. Remember, it is your subconscious mind's duty to protect and preserve you. Once you are fully committed to your plan of action, it has no choice but to help because without its help, you may fail, which would be counter to your subconscious mind's mission to protect you from embarrassment and humiliation.

To make sure our subconscious mind understands that we are fully committed to our plan, we must make that commitment very clear. Unlike William the Conqueror, we can't do something as dramatic as burn the boats. Instead, we must put some "skin in the game." We all understand the theory, "It is okay to fail . . . so long as no one else knows we have failed." The corollary to that is, "It is not okay to fail if others have become aware of our plan." The more people who know of our plans, the less okay it becomes to fail. As the number of people who are aware of our plans increases, so does the embarrassment, humiliation, and pain that we will suffer if we subsequently fail in this quest. Our subconscious mind will do everything in its power to make sure that doesn't happen.

Achieving significant objectives requires significant commitment. The level of commitment rises in direct proportion to the number of people who we make aware of our promise.

While this kind of pressure may seem like an undue hardship, it really isn't. After all, aren't you planning on succeeding? If you are worried about the risk of failure, you are already conceding that you might fail, which means that your chances of success have been greatly reduced—before you even start! These inconsistent signals (telling yourself you are going to accomplish your objective and at the same time, being afraid you might fail) are like trying to drive your car with one foot on the brake pedal and the other foot on the gas pedal. If you are applying the same amount of pressure on the gas pedal as you are the brake pedal, you are not going to make much progress. If you are afraid to go forward, leave your foot firmly on the brake pedal. If, however, you really do want to go forward, you must take your foot off of the brake pedal.

There are three other very substantive reasons why you should tell people about your promise and your intention to accomplish it.

1. Other people will help you accomplish your promise.

Regardless of the size and shape of our personal objective, we always need the help and cooperation of others to accomplish it. No one has ever accomplished an objective by himself or herself. Every worthwhile objective I have ever seen accomplished required some assistance by someone other than the person who set the target.

If your objective is a personal objective, you will need the help, assistance, cooperation, or at least the moral support of your spouse, your family, and/or your friends.

If your promise is a business-related promise, you will absolutely need the help of your employees. No business enterprise ever accomplished a corporate objective without the help and assistance of the employees. Anyone who thinks a business accomplishes its objectives because of the CEO or senior management is sadly mistaken. Yes, the CEO and senior management must do their jobs, but if the employees don't help, no CEO or senior management can make up the difference.

The people you tell about your promise become a resource for assistance. If these people are not aware of our objective, how can they possibly assist us?

Let me give you an example of how important it is to get people to help you—and how much you can accomplish when a group of people work with you in pursuing your promise.

In 1995, when my company only had 150 employees and annual revenues of $20 million, I called all of the employees together for a company-wide meeting to tell them my vision for the future of our company. After they settled into their seats, I promised them that our company would be a $1 billion revenue company with 5,000 employees by the year 2000.

Now that was a pretty outlandish statement. I had promised to increase revenues by fifty times our historical high in the next five years. And if that weren't enough, I had also said I was going to increase our staffing by twenty-seven times in the same period of time.

Fortunately for me, the vast majority of my employees were not only a tremendous group of hard-working, dedicated employees, they had also been introduced to the principles of this book during their initial training program.

I was so confident that we would accomplish this promise that I had the tail numbers (each aircraft has a unique FAA registration number painted on its tail) on our jet airplane changed to read "KB152." The "K" was the first initial of my wife's name, and the "B" was the first initial of my name. The "1" stood for the $1 billion in revenue, the "5" stood for the 5,000 employees, and the "2" stood for the year 2000.

I not only made this promise in front of 150 people (whose help I needed), I also painted the promise on the tail of the jet, so I would see it every time I boarded that aircraft.

Three years later—not five years as promised—we hit annual revenues of $1 billion. By that same three-year mark, we had grown to 4,000 employees. None of that would have been possible without the hard work and determination of each one of those employees.

Once you tell your spouse, your family, your friends, your co-workers, and the others who can provide some type of assistance or moral support, one of two things will inevitably happen. These people will quickly fall into one of two categories:

Those who will support you.

I personally believe that mankind is good and that people will generally strive to do the right thing. Helping someone who has requested our assistance is the "right thing" to do—and most people will respond positively to such a request. It has been said that the highest compliment you can pay someone is to genuinely seek his or her opinion. Think of how you feel when someone asks you for your opinion, for your suggestion, or for your help. Most often you will feel flattered. It is no different for the people you ask.

Those who will laugh at you.

Sadly, there is another kind of people on this planet. This other kind of people is comprised of the small, insecure people who measure their success by how much success you have. If you have more than they have, they become jealous and spiteful. They don't want you to succeed because if you do, they will look bad by comparison.

These people will tell you that your promise is stupid, unattainable, or not worth the effort. They will act like your friend while they are doing everything they can to keep you from becoming better than they are. These are the same people who think, "All successful people are either liars, cheaters, or crooks—or they just got lucky."

We have all met people like this in our lifetime. It is sad to see such a waste of humanity, as these people will spend their whole life complaining about why life just isn't fair. They will have an excuse for why they are where they are. Almost always, they will blame their condition on someone or something—ranging from their parents to their spouse to their kids to the president to the economy. To them, it doesn't matter who they blame so long as they have someone besides themselves to blame for their station in life.

Frequently, people will ask me how they should deal with people like this. My answer is always the same: "You should forgive and ignore ignorance." I am not offering the term "ignorance" in a hateful or condescending sense but rather to reflect a lack of knowledge or a lack of awareness. I would like to believe that people like this aren't bad people; instead, they are people who just don't know any better. All you can do is forgive their ignorance and simultaneously ignore their advice and their ignorance.

Regardless of how you personally choose to deal with these types of people in your life, there are two things you absolutely must do:

- Ignore their advice.

- Don't let any of their negative comments get recorded in your file cabinet. As we discussed in chapter two, when you check any of their comments for factual accuracy, you will be able to discount whatever it is they have said as unfounded, biased, and inaccurate.

2. Telling others about your promise will make you learn to articulate—specifically the what, why, where, when, and how—of your promise.

The second reason for telling people about your promise and your intention to accomplish it is that knowing you have to tell others will require you to define and articulate your promise.

It is one thing to write your promise on a piece of paper; it is quite another thing to verbalize it to someone else. When you are writing your ideas on your promise plan, you already know what you are thinking, so it doesn't matter if your words are not a full and complete description. When you tell someone else, you will need to fully communicate not only the what, but the why, when, where, and how.

As you tell others about your promise, they will have questions for which you will either need to have an answer or be able to find an answer. This process of having to explain (and in some cases defend or persuade) will sharpen your focus and bring to your attention impediments that need to be overcome or solutions that you otherwise might not have found. Either way, you will have gained by the experience.

3. The people you tell become a motivator to keep you going.

Now that you have shared this promise with others, they too have become personal motivators for you. The fear of letting them down—or having to tell them you failed—becomes a new and additional incentive to succeed.

Each time you review your promise plan, add to the "personal motivators" section the name of any person with whom you have shared your plans. By adding more names to this section, you are reinforcing your likelihood of success. You are giving your subconscious even more reasons why it cannot let you fail.

When we discussed the pocket promise, I suggested you have two dozen of these printed. You should give each person that you tell about your promise one of your pocket promise cards.

Mastermind

Over eighty years ago, Napoleon Hill, in his classic self-help book entitled *The Laws Of Success,* introduced the world to the term "mastermind." Napoleon Hill tells the story of how Henry Ford, Thomas Edison, Harvey Firestone, and a handful of other very successful and prominent businessmen of the late eighteenth and early nineteenth centuries would gather on a regular occasion to help each other with their respective business issues. During these sessions, one of the members would identify his particular problem or issue. During the balance of the session, all of the participants would offer their advice and recommendation on how to accomplish the task or solve the problem. Napoleon Hill termed this process the "mastermind" because the solutions that flowed from this process were not just the product of one mind but rather the minds of all those in attendance. Hill went on to explain that the power wasn't just that these were all very, very smart businessmen. It was something more than that. By all of them working together in concert with a mutual objective of truly helping each other, they created a process that produced results that not one of them alone could have produced. This is a classic example of where "the whole becomes greater than the sum of the parts."

Some people might shy away from the term "mastermind" under the mistaken belief that it implies something mystical, which it does not. The modern day version of this same process is frequently referred to as a "board of advisors."

Whether you call your group a mastermind or a board of advisors is absolutely immaterial. It isn't the name that is important; it is the function they will help you accomplish that matters most. You will not only receive great advice, you will also find yourself hanging out with successful, positive people rather than negative people. Instead of being pulled down by negative comments, thoughts, and suggestions, you will be pushed up by positive comments, thoughts, and suggestions.

Identify a small group of people who have demonstrated the qualities you admire. Arrange a personal visit with each, and at this meeting, explain your promise and ask if he or she would be willing to meet with you and a few others one night (day) a month for a few hours. At this first meeting, show the individual your promise plan to demonstrate your sincerity and commitment to the process. You will be amazed by the helpful response you receive.

I have utilized this concept in every business venture in which I have been engaged over the past forty years. It has produced tremendous results for me. By sharing my problems and concerns with people who have remarkably different backgrounds and different areas of expertise, I have been able to tap into ideas and solutions that I would have been incapable of accomplishing by myself.

RULE # 9:

Envision the Result.

*The third eye—when you see things as finished product[s]
way before [they] happen.*

—Arnold Schwarzenegger

*A man can succeed at almost anything for which he has
unlimited enthusiasm.*

—Charles Schwab

The impossible: what nobody can do—until somebody does.

—Anonymous

I've seen this movie before—I know how it ends.

—Bill Bartmann

It is kind of fun to do the impossible.

—Walt Disney

Set your mind on things above.

—Colossians 3:2

Mental vision is the ability of the human mind to display and record an event in a person's mind as if this event has actually occurred, when in fact it has not yet occurred. Depending on the amount of emotional significance associated with the exercise, this event is displayed (and recorded) in three-dimensional living color with sound and action. The sound, color, and acting in this production rival anything yet produced by Hollywood. This display is so realistic because our mind can go to its internal film library and produce real sights, real sound, and real smells that we have previously experienced—as we actually experienced them. Our mind then has the additional power to make these mental pictures conform to the role it has assigned each person in this melodrama within our mind. It assigns a particular script to each of the actors, telling them what to say and how to say it.

The most identifiable example of this process is demonstrated in the phenomena most people refer to as "worry." Worry (a subpart of fear) is the misuse of imagination. With worry, we use our mental vision to see and feel negative things—things that have not yet occurred but that we are afraid might happen. As we worry, we begin to see, feel, and hear the result of this negative that has not yet occurred. As our worry level increases, so does our sense perception, and our mental vision becomes even more realistic. We see, feel, and hear the dreaded result coming to pass—in living color, with all of the appropriate cast of characters present, each one saying or acting out the very consequence we feared.

When we engage in worry, we are acting "as if" the bad or negative thing that we fear might happen has already happened. Along with seeing, feeling, and hearing this thing as if it has already happened, we are attaching whatever emotional reaction is accompanying the feeling. Did you ever wake up in the middle of the night in a cold-sweat or startle yourself awake because of something you were worried about? It could have been a worry about your relationship with someone else, or your fear of losing your job, or of not getting the promotion, or of not being able to pay your bills. Of course you have! We all have had one of these worry thoughts during our sleep that was so real—so scary—that it actually woke us. If these worry thoughts can create that kind of physical change (wake us out of a sound sleep), you can only imagine the strength of the emotional reaction that was attached to such a thought. Likewise, when we have these or similar worry thoughts during the day—when we are wide awake and our palms begin to sweat or we feel our stomach getting queasy—we know there is a significant emotional attachment being associated with the thoughts we are now experiencing.

The picture we are seeing in our mind—complete with all of the sights, sounds, images of people, and the ongoing conversations—is a figment of our imagination. Yet every time we worry and have an emotional reaction to the worry, we are adding more negative data to our file cabinet, and amazingly, this thing we are worrying about hasn't even happened! The very events we are experiencing in our mind not only have not happened but perhaps they never will happen.

We humans are so quick to act "as if " when it comes to a negative, and feel that to do so is perfectly normal, yet when we try to act "as if" on a positive thought, we feel like we are just playing a little game in our mind, and that it is strange of us to do so. It really is the very same process. Isn't this attitude both silly and illogical? Of course it is! In both cases, we will do the exact same things:

1. We will spend time thinking about something that has not yet happened.

2. We will be thinking about this future event as vividly as we can.

3. We will add all of the sights and sounds, and even as much of the anticipated conversation as we can muster.

4. We will simultaneously attach as much emotional reaction as we can to the thoughts we are experiencing.

5. Our mind will enter the data in our file cabinet for quick and easy retrieval.

Why is it okay to do this for a negative thought but not okay to do this for a positive one?

We can use our mental vision to feel the results of accomplishing our objective before it has actually been achieved. As we engage in mental vision, we are bombarding our senses with the feeling of success. This internally generated data becomes real to the memory bank of the mind and will be filed as an event that really occurred. As such, it will be one of the pieces of information that the mind will recall when it inquires as to whether we are capable of accomplishing our objective.

Tiger Woods uses this technique before every golf shot. In the book, *Think Like Tiger* by John Anrisani, Tiger explains how he engages in mental vision prior to each and every shot. During his practice swing, Tiger mentally watches the club's head hit the ball and the ball leave the club's head. His mental vision doesn't end there; he continues to visualize not only the trajectory of the ball while in flight but also how it will roll once it lands on the ground. Only after he has seen this complete picture will he perform the actual shot. How can your mind help you accomplish what you want unless it knows what it looks like? Once your subconscious mind "sees" what it is you want, it will figure out what it needs to do to help you achieve it.

Kathy and I used a technique to help get us through law school. While we were in law school, we lived in married student housing—a twelve-foot wide, forty-foot long cement block apartment. This was a four-story building with each apartment—about the shape and size of a singlewide mobile home—stacked one on top of the other. In addition to taking out student loans to cover some of the tuition, we both worked forty-hour-a-week jobs to buy groceries and pay the balance of the tuition and book bills. We didn't have any extra money for entertainment, so our social life for the full three years of law school consisted of going to the Mexican food restaurant across the street from our apartment on Friday nights. Since our budget was limited, we would each order a single taco. If we had had a particularly successful week, we'd really go crazy and buy a third taco and split it.

To convince ourselves that all of this hard work and sacrifice was worth the effort, we would hop into our car and drive through the rich neighborhoods in Des Moines, Iowa. There was one particular street named Tonawanda Drive that had what we thought were the most luxurious houses we had ever seen. As we would drive up and down Tonawanda Drive, we would decide which house we liked better than the others and what we would do to it if we owned it. We acted as if we had the capacity to purchase any house in the area and that we were being selective because we wanted to make sure we were making a good purchase. This technique worked for both of us. Whenever we would get disillusioned with school or with life in general, we'd hop into the car and go get a dose of positive motivation. We knew that if we successfully completed law school, we would be positioned to live such a lifestyle.

KEY POINTS

1. Before you set your objective or decide what you want to become, do, or have . . . make sure it is your objective and not someone else's. You are not here to live up to others' expectations of you; you are here to live up to your expectations of you.

2. Don't call your objective a goal, call it a promise. A promise carries deep emotional attachment and will cause your mind to give it priority filing.

3. Clearly identify your objective. In order to hit a target, you must first see it clearly.

4. Identify your personal motivator. Determine why you want to achieve, become, or have this objective you have labeled your promise. Create a personal reminder that you can view daily to reinforce and to reinvigorate you.

5. Create a promise plan, This promise plan needs to contain a clear and concise statement of your promise, along with the details of the WHEN, WHERE, WHY, HOW, and WHO of accomplishing this promise.

6. Review your promise regularly. Put your promise plan in a location where you will come in contact with it every couple of weeks. Put it with your checkbook or in the same location where you temporarily store your monthly bills until it is time to pay them.

In addition to your promise plan, also find some visual reminder of your promise, and put that where you will see it frequently, if not every day.

For example, put your visual reminder:

- On the bedroom wall.

- On a bathroom mirror.

- Under the glass on your desk.

- In your notebook.

- On your desk.

- In a picture frame on your desk.

- Next to your phone.

Carry your laminated pocket promise with you every day. If you do, you will see it at minimum twice a day: once in the morning when you are putting it in your pocket and once in the evening when you are taking it out of your pocket.

7. It is not only important that you believe you can accomplish your objective, it is also important to tell yourself that you will accomplish your objective. This positive affirmation becomes a source of data that your mind can now call upon if and when it develops doubts about the accomplishing this objective.

8. Tell others of your promise. Telling others your promise increases your commitment. It also enables you to enlist the help and support of those you will need to assist you in accomplishing your promise.

9. We can use our mental vision to feel the results of accomplishing our objective before it has actually been achieved. As we engage in mental vision, we are bombarding our senses with the feeling of success. This internally generated data becomes real to the memory bank of the mind and will be filed as an event that really occurred. As such, it will be one of the pieces of information that the mind will recall when it inquires as to whether we are capable of accomplishing this objective.

Chapter Four

RIGORS
OF EXERCISE

Don't get tired of doing what is right, for in due season you shall reap if you don't faint.

—Galatians 6:9

Genius is 1 percent inspiration and 99 percent perspiration.

—Thomas Edison

Nothing in the world can take the place of persistence.
Talent will not; nothing is more common than unsuccessful men with talent.
Genius will not; unrewarded genius is almost a proverb.
Education will not; the world is full of educated derelicts.
Persistence and determination alone are omnipotent.

—Calvin Coolidge

Dreams don't work unless you do.

—Peter Daniels

Don't tell yourself how big your problems are—tell your problems how big you are.

—Bill Bartmann

One of these days—is none of these days.

—English Proverb

We have learned the nine rules necessary to accomplish any objective. While knowledge of these nine rules is crucial, simply knowing the rules will not make your objective happen. Just because we know the rules of golf or the game of basketball doesn't make us a better golfer or a better basketball player. If we wish to be a better golfer or a better basketball player in addition to knowing the rules, we will need to practice and hone our golf and basketball skills.

It is the same way for us if we want to be proficient in accomplishing our objectives. If we wish to possess a sharp, creative mind with an unstoppable positive attitude, we can, but as a precondition, we must perform the exercises that will create such a mind.

We have all heard and even seen examples of the ninety-eight pound weakling who was so dissatisfied with his physical condition and the limitations this condition put on him that he committed to change this physical condition. His desire to change could have been based on either a positive or negative motivation. He could have been tired of being threatened or humiliated by the neighborhood bully (negative), or had a desire to be healthy and live longer, or hoped to impress the girl of his attention (positive). For purposes of this discussion, it doesn't matter whether his motivation was positive or negative. What was important was that he was motivated and that he took affirmative action to accomplish his objective.

As he began his weight training, body building, calisthenics, and any other form of physical exercise he deemed necessary to accomplish his objective—whether muscle gain, strength, endurance, or otherwise—he picked the exercise capable of accomplishing his specific target. He took affirmative action and stuck with it until the result was accomplished.

We have seen this same phenomena a thousand times in our own life. We read about it every day in the sport section of our daily newspaper. If you doubt this, open today's newspaper to the sports section and read the stories about professional athletes.

Depending upon the season, you will see a golfer shooting a subpar round of golf, a baseball pitcher throwing a no-hitter, a quarterback throwing a record number of passes without an interception, a track star setting a new speed distance record, a boxer scoring a first round knockout, or a bowler rolling a 300 game. These examples are there every day, yet we fail to learn the lesson they should teach us. The lesson is so obvious, it is often overlooked. Instead of noticing what should have been so obvious, we say, he was lucky or he had a lot of natural talent. Professional athletes may modestly refer to their luck or thank God for their natural talent while being interviewed by the press, but they know the truth. The truth is that luck and natural talent have little to do with their success. They know that the real reason for their success is simply that they have set an objective, have taken affirmative action steps to accomplish this objective, and have stuck with it no matter how hard or boring it became. They decided what they wanted. They took the steps necessary to achieve it. They practiced continuously. They picked the exercises they knew would enhance performance—whether it was hitting a baseball, a golf ball, or a tennis ball—and they practiced this exercise hundreds of times each day. A professional athlete eats, drinks, and sleeps his sport. He is constantly aware of it and is always looking for new and better ways to improve his performance. He becomes entirely devoted to accomplishing his objective.

A recent survey of professional athletes revealed the amount of practice the average member of the following professions devotes to practicing his or her game:

- PGA golfers: two to three hundred practice balls per day, every day.

- NBA basketball players: forty to sixty hours per week.

- Marathon runners: twenty to thirty hours per week.

Some people reading this survey probably said, "No wonder they are so good; they practice all the time." Well, now isn't that an interesting statement? Think about it for a minute. That is exactly why they are so good. They have learned that they need to practice regularly to get good and stay good. Yes, they have talent and skill, but even with talent and skill, they know they need to practice constantly.

Think of the sport you use as recreation. It doesn't matter whether it is golf, baseball, basketball, tennis, or bowling. Now spend a minute thinking of how much better the professional athlete who plays this particular sport is at it than you are. Now try to imagine how much better you would be if you had a professional coach, expensive training equipment, and an unlimited amount of time to practice every day. Assuming you had no physical disabilities, you would improve tremendously, and with the right combination of these three things, you could play reasonably competitively with any of the professional athletes.

The only major difference between you and professional athletes is that they have picked a particular sport as their occupation. Their ability to succeed and, therefore, to produce the level of income they have determined they want is 100 percent dictated by the results they produce. The results they produce are entirely dictated by the amount of time and effort they spend sharpening their skills.

Isn't the same really true of each of us? If this is so, then shouldn't we commit the same effort and energy to accomplishing what we want as an athlete commits to his endeavor? Our efforts and energies shouldn't be focused on hitting golf balls or throwing baseballs; they should be expended on the one thing that can help us accomplish our objective—building positive self-image.

Positive thinking does indeed work when it is consistent with the individual's self-image. It literally cannot work when it is inconsistent with one's self-image (or at least until the self-image itself has been changed).

ERGO: Positive thinking is the second step. A positive self-image is the first—and therefore most important—step.

Self-image is the base upon which we build our future. A strong base will withstand a few setbacks as minor inconveniences. A weak base, however, will crumble at the first appearance of conflict or possibility of failure.

At the first sign of trouble, the self-image looks to itself for instructions on how to react to the situation at hand. If it detects a strong self-image that is confident of handling the situation that has been presented, it becomes calm and assured, knowing this situation is only a minor problem. It puts this new problem in proper perspective and spends only the amount of time this particular situation truly warrants.

If, however, it detects a weak self-image, its anxiety level increases, and the problem is allowed to grow out of proportion with reality. To make matters even worse, this lack of security now lets the mind run helter-skelter, imagining all sorts of negative complications and ramifications that might occur if this problem is not solved promptly. Now, rather than calmly dealing with one minor issue, the mind is forced to solve many larger and much more complicated issues, all the while being pushed beyond its own abilities for an immediate answer. If the mind can't come up with a quick, solid answer (and it can't because most of the problems it is trying to solve don't even exist), the anxiety grows even larger as we now begin to even doubt our ability to solve a little problem. This is when panic, stress, and depression enter. Our incorrectly perceived inability to solve the problem has shattered our self-confidence and deflated our self-image. We now begin to think that we are incapable of fending for ourselves and, hence, are at the mercy of whatever comes down the road.

KEY POINTS

1. Knowledge of the nine rules is crucial if we want to learn how to improve our self-image.

2. In addition to knowing the nine rules, we must also practice the exercises until we become proficient at them.

3. Self-image is the base upon which we build our future. A strong base will withstand a few setbacks as merely minor inconveniences. A weak base, however, will crumble at the first appearance of conflict or possibility of failure.

4. Positive thinking does indeed work when it is consistent with the individual's self-image. It literally cannot work when it is inconsistent with one's self-image (or at least until the self-image itself has been changed).

   ERGO: Positive thinking is the second step. A positive self-image is the first—and therefore most important—step.

Chapter Five

CHANGE THE WAY YOU VIEW YOURSELF

*What lies behind us and what lies before us are tiny matters compared
to what lies within us.*

—Ralph Waldo Emerson

*It is not because things are difficult that we dare not venture, it is because
we dare not venture that things are difficult.*

—Seneca

Get it right in your head—and you'll get it right in your life.

—Bill Bartmann

Greater is he who is in me than he who is in the world.

—John 4:4

Someone else's opinion of me—does not change my opinion of me.

—Bill Bartmann

The most common cause of failing to achieve a stated objective is the inability to deal with self-doubt. When we first embark on the path to achieve a new objective, we are excited and charged up. We are truly and fully motivated. We see and feel the target toward which we are striving and have all the confidence in the world that we will achieve our ambition. Thereafter (and sometimes, only shortly thereafter), we begin to lose this emotional excitement and realize we are going to have to work hard to accomplish this goal. Our euphoric mood begins to weaken as we start seeing impediments or road blocks in the path to our goal. As the emotional excitement begins to fade and the pragmatic realization of the hard work facing us begins to grow, our self-preservation instinct kicks into overdrive.

It is during these moments of self-doubt that our subconscious mind begins to go through the file cabinets looking for data that will cause it to believe this objective can be accomplished—or not be accomplished. If it finds more positive data than negative data, it will believe that this objective can be accomplished and will continue forward in an effort to achieve it. If, on the other hand, it finds more negative data than positive data, it will assume the objective may not be attainable, and rather than plow forward and end up in failure (which is inconsistent with its mission for us), it begins its attempt to talk us out of pursuing this objective.

Anyone who has ever attempted to quit smoking or to stay on a diet knows how fast good intentions can fade once the urge to have a cigarette or have something to eat strikes. What most of these people didn't know, however, was that this battle wasn't decided by willpower as is commonly misunderstood but rather was decided by the information accessed by our subconscious mind.

Although not being able to quit smoking and not being able to lose weight are significant health concerns, both of them pale in comparison to a more serious medical problem that is caused by a poor self-image. It is estimated that more than ten million people in America suffer from some form of depression. Most of these people are taking some type of anti-depressant medicine such as Prozac. These drugs are reasonably effective at treating the mood, but it isn't the mood that is the real problem! The real problem is a poor self-image that causes the depressed mood. None of these drugs does a thing to fix the poor self-image that is causing the real problem.

Last year in America, 38,000 people committed suicide and 400,000 people attempted suicide. These people didn't engage in suicidal activities because they felt good about who they were; quite to the contrary, these people engaged in the ultimate act of self-destruction because they couldn't live with the image they had of themselves.

Unless the self-image is improved, our battle to quit smoking, our battle to lose weight, our battle to end depression-driven mood swings, our battle to resist suicide, and all of the other battles we want to fight to improve our lives will have the same unsatisfactory result we have had to date.

So how do we change a poor self-image to a strong self-image? Very simply . . .

We tell our mind the truth!
We really are better than we think we are!!!!!

Now that is a strong statement—but I am going to prove it to you. Once I do, you will be able to begin to change your life.

For way too many years, we have been taught to be modest. We have been taught to downplay our successes, and at the same time, we were taught to make a big deal out of our failures. During that time, our file cabinet didn't get very much good news because we didn't attach much emotional reaction to our successes—mostly in an effort to be modest. And at the same time, we did add emotional reaction to virtually every single drop of bad news that came within reach (real or imagined).

Over the course of our life, we have had plenty of successes, victories, accomplishments, acknowledgements, awards, and praises, but our mind has not given these good things fair treatment. Our mind isn't being unfair because it wants to be mean or evil. No, quite simply, our mind has treated these good things as less significant than bad things based on the instructions we sent when these events happened. Our mind didn't give our positive experiences fair treatment because we didn't attach much (if any) emotional reaction to these good things compared to the amount of emotional reaction we attached to the negatives we have also suffered during our life. Our mind has been unfair with us because of our modesty. Our modesty, and our "aw shucks, it was no big thing" attitude caused us to attach little or no emotional reaction to our good thing experiences.

Most of our successes, our victories, our accomplishments, and our acknowledgements all went into the warehouse of our mind with little or no emotional reaction attached to them. Subsequently, they ended up in that vast pile of data strewn across the warehouse floor. These good things really did happen and our mind really did receive the information. The problem, however, is that it didn't put this good news into our file cabinet for quick retrieval; instead, it put it out there with all of the other stuff we have experienced over the course of our lifetime. Our good stuff has become the veritable needle in the haystack out in the middle of the warehouse.

When our mind searches for data to determine whether it thinks we can safely (and not suffer failure, defeat, embarrassment, or humiliation) accomplish a particular task, it finds plenty of negative data in our file cabinet. If it doesn't find enough positive data to balance out the negative, it will conclude that it should discourage us from attempting this task.

Many times, if our mind had looked beyond the file cabinet and had rooted around out there in that big pile of stuff on the warehouse floor, it would have found enough good stuff to outweigh the negatives in our file cabinet. If it had gone this extra step, it would have returned with an entirely different conclusion regarding our ability to accomplish a particular task, and it would have begun to assist us in the effort—instead of doing the exact opposite.

The difference in the conclusion arrived at by the subconscious mind isn't determined by how many successes or failures we have actually had during our lifetime but rather by which information our mind selectively chose to use when it sought the answer to its question.

Just because we failed to attach emotional reaction to a long-past event doesn't mean we have to continue to suffer as a result. It is not too late to add these positives to our file cabinet so that when our mind searches through our file cabinets in the future, it will fairly consider both the positives we have experienced as well as the negatives. Once our mind gives fair consideration to both sides, we have a good chance of winning.

So how do we fix this problem and belatedly get these good things into our file cabinet? The next time our mind asks a question about our chance of success, we want our mind to have more good things to help out-balance the negative things.

We don't need some mystical incantation nor some voodoo or black magic. We don't need to believe in any hocus-pocus. This is not some sleight-of-hand technique to fool our mind. We don't need to be in denial about what has happened in our life. We don't need to wish away or attempt to rationalize things that have occurred. We don't have to create, manufacture, or make up some fantasy. All we have to do is be honest with ourselves.

Very simply, we have to go out on to that warehouse floor and root around until we find all of our positive experiences—all of our previous successes, accomplishments, acknowledgments, awards, and kudos. Once we find them, we need to dust them off and put them in our file cabinet. If we can find them and then put them into our file cabinet, they will be available for consideration the next time our subconscious mind seeks an answer to that question.

Here is how we do it. We go out on that warehouse floor to look for our prior good things by doing the following exercise. This exercise simply consists of making a list of all of the good things you have done, felt, or experienced over the course of your life. Now before you roll your eyes and grimace about having to do a drill that you aren't sure will really help you, let me tell you that I have engaged in this simple exercise all of my life. It has taken me from being a high school dropout to becoming a lawyer. It has taken me from having a fifth grade reading level as a junior in high school to becoming a college instructor. It has taken me from a traveling carnival to a permanent place in the Smithsonian Institute. It has taken me from poverty to becoming a millionaire. It has taken me from a minimum wage job to a position that paid me millions of dollars a year. It has taken me from riding the city bus to flying my own $25 million jet aircraft. It has taken me from homeless to a 12,000 square foot home. It has taken me from drawing unemployment to employing over 4,000 people. It has taken me from a million dollars in debt to over a billion dollars to the good. It has taken me from a workaholic to a devoted husband. I can't yet know what your *promise* is for yourself, but I am willing to bet it is somewhere within the range of things that this exercise has already accomplished for me. I believe in this exercise so strongly that I still continue to revise my list as I find new good things on my warehouse floor. I carry my list with me every single day of my life.

I have been teaching this technique for the past twenty years. I have had the opportunity to teach the technique of finding the good data in our brain's warehouse to thousands of people, and I have watched it transform the lives of those who took it seriously and followed these four steps.

STEP ONE: FIND YOUR PRIOR POSITIVE EXPERIENCES.

The first step in this process is to search through that pile of stuff in the middle of your warehouse floor to find the good things that really did happen in your life. Amazingly, these good things are going to be easy to find. Even though they didn't get recorded with emotional attachment and even though they are scattered with a bunch of other data out there on our warehouse floor, we are going to be able to perform our own search and rescue mission to find this helpful data. This job is going to be easier than anyone ever would have imagined because of the tool we are going to use to accomplish it. Our mind is a fabulous and powerful supercomputer capable of performing functions almost beyond description. We are going to enlist the help and support of that supercomputer to help us sort through all of that stuff piled up on our warehouse floor.

All we have to do is to tell it where to look.

Over the course of the past twenty years, as I have taught this method to thousands of people, I have found it helpful to allow your mind to proceed in a logical and orderly fashion. The worksheets that follow are designed to stimulate thought and to allow our supercomputer mind to begin to focus on the specific pile of data from each particular time frame of our life, rather than just root around through the entire warehouse.

As you read each question, spend a moment or two thinking about the question being asked. Don't be in a hurry to proceed to the next question; this exercise can and will change the rest of your life if you do it slowly and thoughtfully. The amount of time you spend doing this exercise will bear a direct relationship to how much benefit you will receive. Go slowly, and spend time thinking about each question. If you need to put your feet up and close your eyes as you think about the question, then do so.

Before you begin, let me tell you that it is extremely important for you to be honest, not modest. Remember, it was our modesty that got us into this situation in the first place. No one besides you is ever going to see the answers you have written down. So don't try to act modest. Be honest, and answer the questions as if your future depended upon it—and it may!

Each item should be interpreted in the light most favorable to you. The choice of interpretation is yours, so why choose the negative if objectively, the positive is just as supportable? I am not suggesting that you should lie to yourself. I am only asking you to forget this stupid thing called "false modesty" and to interpret each item in the most positive light possible.

As you think about each question, scribble the first thoughts that come to mind in the space available or on the margins of the page of this book. If you would rather not deface the book, or if you simply would like to do this exercise on larger worksheets designed for this process, they are available on our Web Site. You may print as many copies of the worksheet pages as you need by downloading them from our Web site at www.billbartmann.com.

As you begin to answer these questions and several different events or thoughts come to mind, write them all down. It doesn't matter in which order they come to mind or in which order you write them down. Don't worry about the spelling, grammar, or punctuation; all you should be focusing on is writing down a description of the answer(s) that pop into your head. When you are finished with the entire drill, you'll come back and rerecord the ones you think are the most important or the most helpful on a separate sheet of paper. For the purpose of this portion of the exercise, all we are trying to do is locate and identify the good things that never made it to our file cabinet, but instead got thrown out onto the warehouse floor.

A. PARENTS, SIBLINGS, AND RELATIVES

Parents:

1 a. What is the best thing either or both of your parents ever said about you?

_____

_____

    b. Which one said it? _____

_____

    c. What did he/she say? _____

_____

    d. Where were you when it happened?_____

_____

    e. Who else was present? _____

_____

    f. What was the occasion? _____

_____

    g. How did it make you feel? _____

_____

2 a. What is the best thing either or both of your parents ever told someone else about you? _____

_____

b. Which one said it? _____

_____

c. What did he/she say? _____

_____

d. How did you find out about it? _____

_____

e. Where were you when you found out about it? _____

_____

f. Who else was present? _____

_____

g. What was the occasion? _____

_____

h. How did it make you feel? _____

_____

3 a. What is the best thing that ever happened to you in front of either or both of
your parents that made you feel really good about yourself? _____
_____

   b. What was it? _____
   _____

   c. When was it? _____
   _____

   d. Which one of your parents (or both) was present? _____
   _____

   e. What did they say to you when it happened? _____
   _____

   f. Who else was present?_____
   _____

4 a. Did your parents ever tell anyone else about what you had done? _____
_____

   b. Whom did they tell? _____
   _____

   c. How did it make you feel? _____
   _____

5 a. What is the best thing you ever accomplished—that your parents know about?

_____

_____

b. What was it? _____

_____

c. When was it? _____

_____

d. How did your parents become aware of your accomplishment? _____

_____

e. What did they say to you when they learned about it? _____

_____

f. Who else was present?_____

_____

g. Did your parents ever tell anyone else about this? _____

_____

h. How did it make you feel? _____

_____

6 a. What was the nicest compliment either of your parents ever gave you? _____

_____

    b. What had you done to receive this compliment? _____

    _____

    c. When was it? _____

    _____

    d. Which one of your parents (or both) was present? _____

    _____

    e. What did they say to you when it happened? _____

    _____

    f. Who else was present?_____

    _____

    g. Did your parents ever tell anyone else about this compliment? _____

    _____

    h. How did it make you feel? _____

    _____

Siblings:

1 a. What is the best thing any of your brothers or sisters ever said about you?

_____

b. Which one said it? _____

c. What did he or she say? _____

d. Where were you when it happened?_____

_____

e. Who else was present? _____

f. What was the occasion? _____

g. How did it make you feel? _____

2 a. What is the best thing any of your brothers or sisters ever told someone else about you? _____

b. Which one said it? _____

c. What did he or she say? _____

d. How did you find out about it? _____

e. Where were you when you found out about it? _____

f. Who else was present?_____

g. What was the occasion? _____

h. How did it make you feel? _____

3 a. What is the best thing that ever happened to you in front of any of your brothers or sisters, that made you feel really good about yourself? _____
_____

b. What was it? _____

c. When was it? _____

d. Which one of your brothers or sisters was present? _____

e. What did he or she say to you when it happened? _____
_____

f. Who else was present?_____

g. Did any of your brothers or sisters ever tell anyone else about what you had done? _____

h. How did it make you feel? _____

4 a. What is the best thing you ever accomplished—that any of your brothers or sisters know about?_____

    b. What was it? _____

    c. When was it? _____

    d. How did your brothers or sisters become aware of your accomplishment?

    _____

    e. What did they say to you when they learned about it? _____

    _____

    f. Who else was present?_____

    g. Did any of your brothers or sisters ever tell anyone else about this? _____

    _____

    h. How did it make you feel? _____

5 a. What was the nicest compliment any of your brothers or sisters ever gave you?

    _____

    b. What had you done to receive this compliment? _____

    _____

    c. When was it? _____

d. What did he or she say to you when it happened? _____

e. Who else was present? _____

f. Did any of your brothers or sisters ever tell anyone else about this compliment? _____

_____

g. How did it make you feel? _____

_____

Relatives:

1 a. What is the best thing any of your relatives have ever said about you?

_____

b. Which one said it? _____

c. What did he or she say? _____

d. Where were you when it happened?_____

e. Who else was present? _____

f. What was the occasion? _____

g. How did it make you feel? _____

2 a. What is the best thing any of your relatives ever told someone else about you?

_____

   b. Which one said it? _____

   c. What did he or she say? _____

   d. How did you find out about it? _____

   e. Where were you at when you found out about it? _____

   _____

   f. Who else was present?_____

   g. What was the occasion? _____

   h. How did it make you feel? _____

   _____

3 a. What is the best thing that ever happened to you in front of any of your relatives that made you feel really good about yourself? _____

_____

   b. What was it? _____

   c. When was it? _____

d. Which one of your relatives was present? _____

e. What did he or she say to you when it happened? _____
_____

f. Who else was present?_____

g. Did your relatives ever tell anyone else about what you had done?_____
_____

h. How did it make you feel? _____

4 a. What is the best thing you ever accomplished—that any of your relatives knows about? _____

b. What was it? _____

c. When was it? _____

d. How did your relatives become aware of your accomplishment? _____
_____

e. What did he or she say to you upon learning about it?_____
_____

f. Who else was present?_____

g. Did your relative ever tell anyone else about this? _____

_____

h. How did it make you feel? _____

_____

5 a. What was the nicest compliment any of your relatives ever gave you? _____

_____

b. What had you done to receive this compliment? _____

_____

c. When was it? _____

d. Which one of your relatives was present? _____

e. What did he or she say to you when it happened? _____

_____

f. Who else was present?_____

g. Did your relatives ever tell anyone else about the compliment? _____

_____

h. How did it make you feel? _____

B. SCHOOL

Grade School:

1 a. What was the best thing that ever happened to you in grade school? _____
_____

    b. What grade were you in when it happened?_____

    c. Who was present?_____

    d. What was said? _____

    e. How did you feel? _____

2. Were you involved in any extra-curricular school functions? (School play, sports, etc.) _____

3 a. What was the best experience you ever had with any of these school functions?
_____

    b. What happened? _____

    c. When did it happen? _____

    d. Where did it happen? _____

e. Who else was present? _____

f. How did it make you feel? _____

4 a. Who was your favorite teacher? _____

b. Why was this teacher your favorite? _____

_____

5. What was the best thing he or she ever said to someone else or said to you—about you? _____

_____

6 a. What was your favorite subject?_____

b. Why was this your favorite subject? _____

c. Did you get good grades in this subject?_____

d. Were you ever called on by the teacher to answer a question, and you got it right? _____

_____

e. How did this make you feel? _____

_____

High School:

1. What was the best thing that ever happened to you in high school?_____
_____

2. Were you involved in any school functions? (school newspaper, yearbook, band, cheerleader, glee club, athletics, academic clubs, school plays, etc.) _____
_____

3 a. What was the best experience you ever had with any of these school functions?
_____

   b. What happened? _____

   c. When did it happen? _____

   d. Where did it happen?_____

   e. Who else was present? _____

   f. How did it make you feel? _____

4 a. Who was your favorite teacher? _____

   b. Why was this teacher your favorite?_____
_____

5 a. What was the best thing he or she ever said to you—about you? _____
_____

   b. What did he or she say? _____

   c. How did this make you feel? _____

6 a. What was the best thing he or she ever said to someone else about you?
_____

   b. What did he/she say? _____

   c. How did this make you feel? _____

7 a. What was your best subject in high school? _____

   b. What kind of grades did you get?_____

   c. Why do you think you did so well? _____

College and Graduate School:

1 a. What was the best thing that ever happened to you in college? _____
_____

   b. When did it happen? _____

   c. Where did it happen?_____

   d. Who else was present? _____

   e. How did you feel? _____ .

2. Were you involved in any school functions? (school newspaper, yearbook, band, cheerleading, glee club, athletics, academic, school plays, etc.) _____
_____

3 a. What was the best experience you ever had with any of these school functions?
_____

   b. What happened? _____

   c. When did it happen? _____

   d. Where did it happen?_____

e. Who else was present? _____

f. How did it make you feel? _____

_____

4 a. Who was your favorite teacher? _____

b. Why was this teacher your favorite? _____

c. What was the best thing he or she ever said to you—about you? _____

_____

d. When did this happen? _____

e. What did he or she say? _____

f. How did this make you feel?_____

5 a. What was the best thing he or she ever said to someone else about you?

_____

b. When did this happen? _____

c. What did he or she say? _____

d. How did this make you feel? _____

_____

6 a. What was your best subject in college? _____

_____

   b. What kind of grades did you get? _____

_____

   c. Why do you think you did so well? _____

_____

7 a. What was your "major" area of study? _____

   b. Why did you pick that one?_____

C. CAREER

1. What is the best thing that ever happened to you at work?_____

_____

2 a. Have you ever been singled out for an award, an acknowledgement, a thank-you, an "attaboy" or "attagirl"? _____

b. When did it happen? _____

c. Who was present?_____

d. What was said? _____

e. Who said it? _____

f. How did you feel?_____

3 a. Have you ever been part of a group, team, section, department, or division that has received an award, an acknowledgement, or a thank-you?_____

_____

b. When did it happen? _____

c. Who was present?_____

d. What was said? _____

e. Who said it? _____

f. How did you feel? _____

_____

4 a. Have you ever received a raise or a promotion? _____

    b. Why did you receive it? _____

    c. Who presented it to you? _____

    d. What did he or she say? _____

    e. Who was present?_____

    f. How did you feel?_____

5 a. Have your co-workers ever sought your advice or recommendation concerning a project? _____

    b. Why do you think they ask you for your advice? _____

    _____

    c. How does this make you feel?_____

    _____

D. SPORTS

1 a. Have your ever participated in any sport activity in grade school, high school, college, or since you finished school? _____

Which ones?_____

_____

For each sport, answer the following questions:

2 a. What is the most exciting, satisfying, or rewarding thing that you have ever experienced while engaging in this sport? (Hole in one, buzzer-beating shot, homerun, game-winning touchdown, strike-out pitch, 300 game, hat trick, ace, etc.)

_____

    b. Where were you when it happened?_____

    c. Who was present?_____

    d. What was said? _____

    e. How did you feel? _____

3 a. Of all the sports in which you have engaged, which is/was your favorite?

_____

    b. Why is/was it your favorite?_____

    c. What is your best memory of any of the times you played this sport?

_____

4 a. Have you ever won any prizes or awards in this sport?_____

_____

    b. When? _____

    c. What was the event?_____

    d. Where was it?_____

    e. Who was present?_____

    f. What was said? _____

    g. How did you feel? _____

5 a. Did you tell anyone about this accomplishment?_____

    b. Who did you tell? _____

    c. How did you feel when you told him or her? _____

_____

    d. What did he or she say? _____

E. CHURCH

1 a. What is the most rewarding experience you have ever had in your church?

_____

b. Who was present? _____

c. How did you feel? _____

F. DATING AND MARITAL RELATIONSHIPS

1 a. What is the best experience you have ever had in your dating or marital relationship? _____

b. What happened? _____

c. When was it? _____

d. Where were you? _____

e. Who was present?_____

f. What was said? _____

g. How did you feel? _____

2 a. What event or situation first convinced you that the other person in this relationship was in love with you? (What picture do you have in your mind when you think of when you first came to this conclusion?)

   b. What happened? _____

   c. When was it? _____

   d. Where were you? _____

   e. Who was present?_____

   f. What was said? _____

   g. How did you feel? _____

3. What event or situation created the most pleasant memory regarding this relationship?_____

4 a. What is the best thing your spouse or significant other ever said about you?

   _____

   b. What did he or she say? _____

   c. Where were you when it happened? _____

d. Who else was present? _____

e. What was the occasion? _____

f. How did it make you feel? _____

5 a. What is the best thing your spouse or significant other ever told someone else about you? _____

b. What did he or she say? _____

c. How did you find out about it? _____

d. Where were you at when you found out about it? _____

e. Who else was present? _____

f. What was the occasion? _____

g. How did it make you feel? _____
_____

6 a. What is the best thing that ever happened to you in front of your spouse or significant other that made you feel really good about yourself? _____
_____

b. What was it? _____

c. When was it? _____

d. What did he or she say to you when it happened? _____

e. Who else was present? _____

f. Did your spouse or significant other ever tell anyone else about what you had done? _____
_____

g. How did it make you feel? _____
_____

7 a. What is the best thing you ever accomplished—that your spouse or significant other knows about? _____

b. What was it? _____

c. When was it? _____

d. How did he or she become aware? _____

e. What did he or she say to you upon learning about it?_____
_____

f. Who else was present?_____

g. Did your spouse or significant other ever tell anyone else about this?

_____

h. How did it make you feel? _____

8 a. What was the nicest compliment your spouse or significant other ever gave you?

_____

b. What had you done to receive this compliment? _____

_____

c. When was it? _____

d. What did he or she say to you when it happened? _____

_____

e. Who else was present? _____

_____

f. Did your spouse or significant other ever tell anyone else about this compliment? _____

_____

g. How did it make you feel? _____

G. CIVIC, CHARITABLE, AND POLITICAL EXPERIENCE

1 a. Have you ever participated in any civic activities such as Girl Scouts, Boy Scouts, YMCA, local libraries, or local boards? _____

    b. In which organization(s) did you participate? _____

_____

    c. What type of activity did you perform? _____

    d. Do you feel that your contribution was helpful to the cause?

_____

    e. Did the organization appreciate your help? _____

    f. How did your participation make you feel? _____

_____

2 a. Have you ever participated in any charitable or fund-raising events?

_____

_____

    b. In which organization did you participate? _____

    c. What type of activity did you perform? _____

d. Do you feel that your contribution was helpful to the cause?

_____

e. Was the organization appreciative of your help? _____

f. How did your participation make you feel? _____

3 a. Have you ever participated in any political events? _____

b. In which organization did you participate? _____

c. What type of activity did you perform? _____

d. Do you feel that your contribution was helpful to the cause?

_____

e. Was the organization appreciative of your help? _____

f. How did your participation make you feel? _____

H. MILITARY EXPERIENCE

1 a. Have you ever been a member of the military? _____

b. In which branch did you serve? _____

c. How long did you serve? _____

2 a. Did you receive any commendations, ribbons, or medals?_____

    b. How did this make you feel? _____

3 a. Did your service make your family and friends proud of you?_____
_____

    b. How do you know they were proud of you? _____
_____

    c. What did they say or do? _____

    d. How did this make you feel? _____

4 a. What was the most rewarding part of your military experience? _____
_____

    b. Where did it happen? _____

    c. Who was there? _____

    d. When did it occur? _____

    e. How did you feel? _____

I. PHYSICAL ATTRIBUTES

1 a. What is your best physical attribute? _____

   b. Why did you pick this one? _____

   c. Has anyone ever complimented you on this attribute? _____

_____

J. FRIENDS AND NEIGHBORS

1 a. What is the nicest thing you have ever done for your friends or neighbors?

_____

   b. Why did you do this?_____

   c. When did you do this? _____

   d. What does your performing this act say about you as a person?

_____

   e. How did you feel when you performed this act for your friends or your neighbors? _____

_____

   f. Did your friends or neighbors know you performed this act on their behalf?

_____

g. What did they say? _____

h. How did you feel? _____

2 a. What is the nicest thing your friends or neighbors have ever done for you?

_____

b. Why do you think they did this for you? _____

c. What does their performing this act for you say about you as a person?

_____

d. How does that make you feel? _____

3 a. What is the best thing any of your friends or neighbors have ever said about you? _____

_____

b. Who said it?_____

c. What did they say? _____

d. Where were you at when it happened?_____

e. Who else was present? _____

f. What was the occasion? _____

g. How did it make you feel? _____

4 a. What is the best thing any of your friends or neighbors ever told someone else about you? _____

b. Who said it?_____

c. What did they say? _____

d. How did you find out about it? _____

e. Where were you when you found out about it? _____

f. Who else was present?_____

g. What was the occasion? _____

h. How did it make you feel? _____

_____

5 a. What is the best thing that ever happened to you, in the presence of your friends or neighbors, that made you feel really good about yourself? _____

_____

b. What was it? _____

c. When was it? _____

d. Where were you when it happened?_____

e. Who was present?_____

f. What did they say to you when it happened? _____

6 a. Did any of your friends or neighbors ever tell anyone else about what you had done? _____
_____

b.How did it make you feel? _____

7 a . What is the best thing you ever accomplished—that your friends or neighbors know about?_____

b. What was it? _____

c. When was it? _____

d. How did your friends or neighbors become aware of your accomplishment?
_____

e. What did they say to you when they learned about it? _____
_____

f. Who else was present?_____

g. Did your friends or neighbors ever tell anyone else about this? _____

_____

h. How did it make you feel? _____

8 a. What was the nicest compliment any of your friends or neighbors ever gave you?

_____

b. What had you done to receive this compliment? _____

_____

c. When was it? _____

d. Where were you? _____

e. Who offered this compliment? _____

f. What did he or she say to you when it happened? _____

_____

g. Who else was present? _____

h. Did your friend or neighbor ever tell anyone else about the compliment?

_____

i. How did it make you feel? _____

K. FINANCIAL

1 a. What has been the most rewarding or satisfying financial transaction in which you have been involved? _____

   b. When did it happen? _____

   c. Who was present?_____

   d. How did it make you feel? _____

2 a. Did you ever tell anyone else about this transaction? _____

   b. How did he or she respond?_____

   c. How did you feel? _____

3 a. Has anyone ever asked your advice or counsel on financial matters?

   _____

   b. Who asked for this advice or counsel? _____

   c. What type of transaction did it involve?_____

   d. When did it happen? _____

e. Who else was present? _____

f. Did this person think you had some knowledge of this type of transaction?

_____

g. Did this person value your opinion and expertise? _____

h. How did this make you feel? _____

L. PERSONAL

1 a. Who was your best friend in high school? _____

b. Why did this person like you so much? _____

_____

2 a. Has anyone ever asked you for your advice, your counsel, or your suggestion on how he or she should handle something happening in life?_____

_____

b. Who was it? _____

c. When did it happen? _____

d. Who else was present? _____

e. How did it make you feel? _____

3. Do you know any foreign languages? _____

4. Do you play any musical instruments? _____

5. Can you sing or dance? _____

Before you answer letters M–U, it is extremely important for me to remind you to be honest, not modest. Remember, it was our modesty that got us into this situation in the first place. No one besides you is ever going to see what you have written down. So don't try to act modest. Be honest, and answer the questions as if your future depends upon it.

M. Name three people who think you are smart.
(1) _____
(2) _____
(3) _____

Why do they think you are smart?
(1) _____
(2) _____
(3) _____

N. Name three people who think you are good-looking or handsome.
(1) _____
(2) _____
(3) _____

Why do they think you are good-looking or handsome?

(1) _____

(2) _____

(3) _____

O. Name three people who think you are fun to be with.

(1) _____

(2) _____

(3) _____

Why do they think you are fun to be with?

(1) _____

(2) _____

(3) _____

P. Name three people who think you are a good person.

(1) _____

(2) _____

(3) _____

Why do they think you are a good person?

(1) _____

(2) _____

(3) _____

Q. Name three people who respect you.

(1) _____

(2) _____

(3) _____

Why do they respect you?

(1) _____

(2) _____

(3) _____

R. If the people who know you well (your family, friends, relatives, co-workers) were to describe your qualities, how many of the following would they say you had?

Honesty? _____

Loyalty? _____

Sincerity? _____

Generosity? _____

Sympathy? _____

Intelligence? _____

Integrity? _____

Ethics? _____

Persistence? _____

Determination? _____

S. Name anyone who has ever said, intimated, or even suggested any of the above (M–R).

_____

T. Of all of the things you have done in your life, of which one are you most proud?

What event was it? _____

Who was present? _____

What was said? _____

How did this make you feel? _____

U. Of all the obstacles you have encountered in your life, which was the hardest to overcome?

What was it? _____

When did it happen? _____

How did you overcome it? _____

How did you feel when you overcame it? _____

V. WRITE YOUR OWN EULOGY.

A eulogy is different than an obituary. An obituary is the short biographical description of the deceased person, written for the newspaper. It says a few nice things about the deceased person but primarily talks about when he/she was born, lived, and died, and how many relatives survive.

A eulogy is very different from an obituary. A eulogy is a speech given at the funeral, the graveside, or at some public forum where the deceased is acknowledged and praised. The purpose of the eulogy is to let everyone in attendance know the lifetime accomplishments and successes of the deceased person. The person giving the eulogy attempts to focus his speech on those things of which the decedent was most proud.

Write your own eulogy, listing the ten things you would want someone to say when he or she describes your lifetime.

1. _____

2. _____

3. _____

4. _____

5. _____

6. _____

7. _____

8. _____

9. _____

10. _____

STEP TWO: Prepare a notable accomplishments list.

The second step in this finding the positive information process is to prepare a list of all of the positive good things that you have found lying around out there on the warehouse floor. I want you to call this list your notable accomplishments, because that is exactly what they are. They are things you have managed to accomplish so far in your life, and each of them is indeed notable. Some may be more notable than others, but they are all notable. As I have said several times, be honest, not modest. If you wrote down the item while you were doing this exercise, you have already answered the question of whether the item is relevant or important. It is! Don't second-guess yourself and decide to leave some of the things you found off of your notable accomplishment list. It was your modesty that got you into this situation; it will be your honesty that gets you out. No one besides you is ever going to see this list, so don't be embarrassed by what you include. Be honest!

As you record these good things on your notable accomplishment list, it isn't important that you put them in any particular order or grouping. It doesn't matter if they are not in chronological order because your mind doesn't store or retrieve things in chronological order. All that is important is that you include all of the good things you discovered during this process. As you begin to list these items, number them in the sequence in which you write them down. Again, it doesn't matter to your mind which of them is first or which of them is last. Your mind will record the fact that a large number of them are based on the numeric length of your list. My notable accomplishment list has fifty numbered items and is three pages long.

STEP THREE: Put the notable accomplishments in the file cabinet.

All of the items on your notable accomplishments list need to get recorded in your file cabinet. Each item on your list is a separate event, and in the future, each will get retrieved separately by your mind. Therefore, it is important that each item gets deposited in your file cabinet—one item at a time.

Here is where a clear understanding of how the mind works becomes crucial. It is because I wanted you to have a clear understanding that I took so much time explaining the process.

The good things you found on the warehouse floor—that have now all been added to your notable accomplishments list—are all items your file clerk has previously seen. When the file clerk saw this data the first time, it did not give that item a priority filing. Your file clerk threw this data out onto the warehouse floor rather than filing it in your file cabinet. We have to make sure your clerk does not make that mistake again.

There are two ways to make sure your file clerk records these notable accomplishments as priority data in your file cabinet, so it can be accessed for quick retrieval. The first way is repetition, and the other is emotion.

REPETITION:

If you were to continuously make the statement, Boy, am I stupid, over a period of time, your mind would accept this statement as true and begin to act accordingly. It really wouldn't matter whether you were actually stupid. Eventually, after hearing it so much and so often, your brain would just accept this flawed observation. That is what the mind does with data it repeatedly hears, even if it is unsure of the truth or falsity of the data it is judging. In our situation, our mind will have a faster and an easier time accepting the truth of each of our notable accomplishments because our mind already knows these events did happen and are true.

To make sure our clerk files these notable accomplishments properly in our file cabinet, we will need to send this message to the clerk repeatedly. We can do this by reviewing our notable accomplishment list on a regular basis. Each time we perform this review, we should think about each item on our list, one at a time. As we think about that one item, we should try to remember the time and the place when the event occurred. The more senses we can involve in the memory, the easier it is for the file clerk to put this data in the right place.

How much repetition does a person have to do before the clerk files this data in the file cabinet? The answer varies from person to person. When I instruct people on this point, I tell them to treat this drill like they would any physical exercise program. The more frequent and more consistent the exercise programs, the faster and better the results. Can a person get beneficial results without a lot of repetition? Yes. Would it be better and faster with repetition? Yes. I tell people that they should do it as often as they can (at least once a day, initially) and then begin to taper off as they feel progress is happening. Once you get this notable accomplishment in your file cabinet, your file clerk is never going to remove it!

The first benefit of repetition is to get your file clerk to file the data in the correct place—the file cabinet. The second benefit of repetition is to increase the importance of the event which moves the data to the front of the file cabinet. Remember, our subconscious mind's quest is to assure the self-preservation of the species. To do that, it is always on the lookout for any data that appears to be significant because it has learned that only significant data can either hurt or help. Consider the earlier statement:

"Boy, am I stupid."

When the subconscious heard that statement the first time, it is very likely it didn't have much, if any, reaction to the statement. As it began to hear that same (otherwise insignificant) statement over and over again, it began to give that insignificant statement a whole new significance. This new significance wasn't because the statement became any more or less significant by itself, but rather because of the mere fact of its repetition. The subconscious mind is not used to hearing something over and over. When it does hear something over and over that in and of itself is unusual.

The mind has been automatically programmed to consider anything unusual as significant. So what happens is that once we get our notable accomplishment in our file cabinet, by continuing with the repetition, we are sending more signals to the file clerk that this is important data. As we continue to send this message to the file clerk, this data takes on an increased sense of importance and moves up the scale in our filing system where it can eventually become the first piece of data the subconscious mind finds when it begins its search.

EMOTION:

Another method to get our file clerk to file each of our notable accomplishments in our file cabinet (rather than on the floor of the warehouse) is to attach emotion to the instruction. The file clerk is automatically programmed to file data with an emotional reaction attached to it as priority information. When this data came through the first time, either the clerk made a mistake or we didn't have very much of an emotional reaction attached to the data. The file clerk can and does make mistakes, especially if the clerk is being bombarded with tons of data all at once and can only process so much at one time. When that happens, the instructions are to record the negative information first and then if there is still time, record the positive. Why would it give negative information a priority over positive information? It is very simple: because that is the best way to guarantee the self-survival of the species.

If our clerk fails to record data that has a negative attached, we may end up repeating that same event and perhaps with greater consequences the second time. If the clerk fails to record data that has a positive attached, it is unlikely that any harm would come to us if that event occurred again. A second reason the clerk may have misfiled this notable accomplishment the first time could be because it showed up at the same time as did some negative data. Again, because of our instinct for self-survival, our negative data almost always has an attached emotional reaction while our positives don't always have one. Even if they do, it may not be as strong as the emotional reaction attached to a negative.

Recently, one of my students shared with me a technique he uses to make sure his file clerk properly files his notable accomplishments in the file cabinet and does not make the same mistake of refiling it out on the warehouse floor. His method is cute and clever—and it does work. He told me that he grew up in a pretty strict home environment in which his mother was the disciplinarian of the family. He said that when he would fail to do something he had previously been told, such as clean up his bedroom or put his dirty clothes in the clothes hamper, his mother would take him by the ear to the job he didn't perform right the first time and make him do it again while she held on to his ear lobe. He went on to tell me that his mother only had to do that one or two times before she made an impression on him that lasted a long time. He said his technique involved the same concept. He said he visualized his mother walking into the warehouse, grabbing the file clerk by the ear, and walking the clerk over to the pile in the center of the floor where that notable accomplishment data had been misfiled. His mother would then instruct the clerk (while holding on to his ear) to pick up the misfiled notable accomplishment and would then walk the clerk (by the ear) all the way back to the door where the file cabinets were located. His mother would continue to hold the file clerk by the earlobe until the clerk had properly filed the notable accomplishment in the very front of the file cabinet.

As I said, it is a cute and clever technique, and it works. Feel free to use this visual or create your own. It doesn't matter which technique you use, as long as you accomplish the mission and get your notable accomplishments in the file cabinet so they can (and will) be retrieved easily and quickly the next time your subconscious mind makes an inquiry.

STEP FOUR: Review the Notable Accomplishments Frequently.

Every time we think about a pleasant, positive experience from our past, we are, in one form or another, reliving it. Our thought might just be a passing glimmer, or it could be a long and thoughtful remembrance of the sights, sounds, and emotions that accompanied the original event. Every time we think this thought, we are sending a brand new signal to our file clerk. Each new signal is one more piece of data for the clerk to have at his disposal when the subconscious mind makes its next inquiry. Because of this, we should make a deliberate effort to review our notable accomplishment list on a frequent basis.

I carry my list of notable accomplishments inside the front cover of a notebook I have with me every day. As a result, there is never a day when I don't have this list within an arm's reach. I have found this list to be a great cure for a "down day" or a "bad day," and yes, we all have down days and bad days. I have them just like you do. They happen to all of us! I have learned that in life we can't always control the things that happen to us, but we can control how we react to them. The most important part of this lesson is not to let bad things go unattended.

When bad things happen, we immediately experience self-doubt. I have learned that self-doubt, if left unattended, quickly turns into anxiety. That anxiety quickly turns into depression, and that depression turns into despondency. This progression downward is like a clump of snow beginning to slide down the mountainside. As it gains speed, it gains weight; as it gains weight, it gathers even more speed, and then more weight, more speed, more weight . . . until this once-harmless snow clump sliding down a slope has become an avalanche with awesome power. This thing that was once nothing more than snow falling from the sky had been allowed to build up until it came loose. When it loosened, it became bigger and stronger. Eventually, what was once nothing more than a solitary snowflake has turned into an avalanche that uproots trees, demolishes houses, and destroys everything in its path. Self-doubt, anxiety, depression, and despondency can destroy everything in our lives.

Our list of notable accomplishments is an effective way to deal with self-doubt. By being honest with ourselves and admitting the mistake, the screw up, or whatever it is that has just happened in our life, we are being honest. We should be equally honest with ourselves by then immediately reminding ourselves of the times when we "didn't make a mistake" and "didn't screw up." We should be honest and balance our failures with our successes. Always, the positives will outweigh and outnumber the negatives.

When I make that last statement in my workshops or in my public speaking, someone frequently challenges me. When that happens, I challenge them to make two lists—the one with all of their notable accomplishments on it and a second one with all of their failures on it. I have now done this with hundreds and hundreds of people from all walks of life, and I have never had one person who was able to list more negatives than positives. The secret to this trick (it is not really a trick, it is just an understanding of how the human mind works) is that I do not make this statement until after one has objectively and honestly prepared the list of notable accomplishments. If I were to make the statement before he or she had finished the list, it would have caused an omission of some of the good things that were recorded on the notable accomplishment drill. Human nature is just that way!

KEY POINTS

1. Our inability to achieve a goal in the past wasn't due to a lack of willpower. It was caused by the information accessed by our subconscious mind.

2. We really are better than we think we are. Our positive experiences do outweigh our negative experiences.

3. Society has taught us to be modest, and our modesty has caused us to downplay our successes and our victories.

4. Our file clerk has not properly filed all our positive experiences in our file cabinet so they can be quickly retrieved by our subconscious mind.

5. We need to be honest with ourselves. We should admit our shortcomings and our mistakes. We should also admit and acknowledge our victories and our successes.

6. We need to search for and locate the prior positive experiences that were not filed properly.

7. We can locate these prior positive experiences by using the worksheets in this chapter.

8. Once we locate and identify these positive experiences, we need to record them on our notable accomplishments list.

9. We then need to make our file clerk refile these positive experiences.

10. We need to review our notable accomplishments list on a regular basis to reinforce our belief in ourself.

WANT TO MAKE A DIFFERENCE IN THE LIVES OF YOUR LOCAL HIGH SCHOOL STUDENTS?

Never doubt that a small group of thoughtful, committed people can change the world. Indeed it is the only thing that ever has.

—Margaret Mead

The National Education Association recently conducted a survey of high school teachers across America. The purpose of the survey was to identify the number one issue for the dramatic increase in teen suicide, teen pregnancy, teen alcoholism, teen drug dependency, and depression.

Although there were a number of factors cited, the survey overwhelmingly pointed to one issue: low self-esteem.

Today's high school students face challenges unlike anything we had to deal with when we were their age. Today's students live in a world that is remarkably different from the one we knew. Their access to information (good or bad) is unparalleled in the history of mankind.

Additionally, today's high school students are growing up in a world where "single-parent" and "dual-income parents" are the norm, not the exception. Subsequently, many of them are learning "values" from their peers, not their parents.

All of this creates an environment in which teens have tremendous amounts of information, very little guidance, and a self-image predicated on peer pressure instead of reality. It is easy to see how such a combination could breed "low self-esteem."

WE CAN CHANGE THIS!
WE CAN HELP THEM RAISE THEIR SELF-ESTEEM!

I make my living traveling the country giving keynote speeches and seminars on the topic of self-esteem. Because my standard one-hour keynote fee is $15,000, my audience generally consists of business groups and trade associations. Likewise, my seminars are generally attended by entrepreneurs of one type or another. Until recently, I had not had the opportunity to give a presentation to high school students.

It only took a couple of those opportunities to cause me to rededicate the balance of my life to a new "mission." Those of you who know me know I am a goal-oriented person. I have been fortunate in my life to have been able to set and achieve a few goals that most people thought were crazy.

I am about to set another "crazy" goal, and I am doing it publicly!

My goal is to put 70,000 high school kids in the Texas Stadium to speak to them about self-respect, self-esteem, peer pressure, and teen suicide.

I want to do this simply because someone should do it, and perhaps it will make a difference. If it prevents one teen suicide or one teen pregnancy, or if it keeps one teenager from becoming dependent on drugs or alcohol, then it will be worth all the effort.

Will this be impossible?   **No!**

Will this be difficult?   **Yes!**

Will this make a difference?   **Absolutely!**

As I set out to accomplish this goal, I know two things:

1. Goals this large don't happen overnight.

This goal will take me several years. It will take hundreds of classroom presentations, followed by hundreds of "full school assemblies," followed by hundreds of "multi-school civic arena presentations" before the "Big Event" can happen.

As I travel the country giving my paid speeches and on my book-signing tour, I will speak for free at the local high schools in each city. I will do this in any city in America so long as I can make the scheduling arrangements.

2. No one accomplishes a goal this large by him or her self.

Big goals require the help of lots of people. To accomplish this goal—and I will accomplish this goal—I will need help from lots of people. In short, I need your help.

I don't need your money—I'll speak for free. I don't even need travel and hotel accommodations because I'll already have both of them as part of the paid keynote speech that gets me to your city.

What I need and what you can provide is an invitation from your local high school to speak to their students. If you know a teacher, a principal, an administrator, or school board members, contact them.

Our kids need someone to help them get through a challenging period in their lives.

Margaret Meade was correct—a small group of people can change the world.

Most people in the world will live and die and never accomplish anything of lasting significance. Yet, all of us have an innate yearning to do something that will "make a difference." Sadly, most people never get the chance—or don't know how.

Here is your opportunity to join me and a "small group of thoughtful, committed people" as we change the world.

WE—you and me and this "small group"—have the chance to do something truly significant. *WE* can change the lives of thousands of young people. *WE* can do for low self-esteem what Betty Ford did for alcoholism and what Susan Komen did for breast cancer.

WE CAN ACCOMPLISH THIS GOAL!

I want you standing beside me on the stage in your high school, of your civic arena, and in the Texas Stadium.

I want you to be able to tell your children and your grandchildren that you were a part of this "small group of thoughtful, committed people" who indeed did change the world!

Pick up the phone and call your local high school.

Once you have a range of dates that work for your school, call me and we'll synchronize schedules. You can call me at (918)388-3328, e-mail me at Bill@billbartmann.com, or go to my Web site www.billbartmann.com.

Afterword

One parting thought. Since this is a book about success, let me share with you my personal definition of success. It may surprise you to find out that my definition of success has nothing to do with money, power, status, prestige, the size of my residence, the type of car I drive, or even the size of my personal jet aircraft. I have chased and caught all of those things, hoping they would make me a success. Over the course of my life, I have learned that while these things are fun to have, they are not the real measure of success. I firmly believe that a person has achieved true success if he or she has three things:

1. Something to do.

2. Someone to love.

3. Something to hope for.

SOMETHING TO DO:

I have something to do. I have made it my personal life's promise to do for failure what Betty Ford did for alcoholism and what Susan Komen did for breast cancer. I want to—by word and example—show people that failure is neither final nor fatal.

I have joined the national speakers' circuit and am telling my story and message of hope and inspiration to audiences across America.

SOMEONE TO LOVE:

Yeah, I have someone to love—my best friend and childhood sweetheart. Kathy and I met when I was fourteen and she was eleven. We dated for ten years and have now been married for thirty-two. Over the past thirty-two years we have had plenty of successes, but none of them has equaled the joy of loving her and knowing that she loves me just as much.

SOMETHING TO HOPE FOR:

I have plenty to hope for. My biggest hope is that I can find a way to carry my message to people who need help overcoming their failures and accomplishing their definition of success. If I can find a way to articulate this message, and then find a way to communicate it in a fashion that they will understand, then my life will have had some true purpose.

A book like this is difficult to end. There is so much more to tell you, so much more to share. I have lived a life that has been rich in experiences. I have been blessed enough to have enjoyed successes that are beyond the comprehension of most people. I have also suffered failures and defeats so bad that I hope no one ever has to suffer the likes of those. After fifty-six years of living the ups and downs of an entrepreneur, I have come to realize that I have found my real purpose in life and that is to share my experiences. I want to share these experiences—not to seek praise, or pity—but rather, to help others reach their goals and to help those who miss their goals to get back up and try again.

If you have plowed your way through this book, you have already demonstrated your persistence—an attribute you will definitely need if you are to accomplish your promise. Your reward for having made it through this book is my genuine offer of assistance. If you have questions or need help, call me or e-mail me. My telephone number is 918-388-3328. My email address is bill@billbartmann.com. If you call me and identify yourself as a person who has read this book, I will take your call if I am in, or I will return your call at the earliest opportunity. Likewise, if you e-mail me, I will respond promptly.